Overturning **Brown**

Overturning BROWN

The Segregationist Legacy
of the Modern
School Choice Movement

STEVE SUITTS

NewSouth Books

Montgomery

NewSouth Books
105 S. Court Street
Montgomery, AL 36104

Library of Congress Cataloging-in-Publication Data

Names: Suitts, Steve, author.
Title: Overturning Brown : the segregationist legacy of the modern school
choice movement / Steve Suitts.
Identifiers: LCCN 2019043214 (print) | LCCN 2019043215 (ebook) |
ISBN 9781588384201 (hardcover) | ISBN 9781588384218 (ebook)
Subjects: LCSH: Segregation in education—United States. | School
choice—Social aspects—United States. | Educational vouchers—United
States. | Educational equalization—United States.
Classification: LCC LC212.52 .S88 2020 (print) | LCC LC212.52
(ebook) | DDC 379.2/63—dc23
LC record available at https://lccn.loc.gov/2019043214
LC ebook record available at https://lccn.loc.gov/2019043215

Design by Randall Williams

Printed in the United States of America by Sheridan Books

NewSouth Books: Suzanne La Rosa, publisher; Randall Williams,
editor-in-chief; Lisa Emerson, accounting manager; Lisa Harrison,
publicist; Matthew Byrne, production manager; Beth Marino, senior
publicity/marketing manager; Kelly Snyder and Isabella Barrera, editorial
and publicity assistants; Laura Murray, cover designer.

To Lynn Walker Huntley
and Sybil Jordan Hampton
Southerners whose wisdom, wit, dedication,
and achievements broke barriers and advanced
equality for all schoolchildren

Contents

Acknowledgments

My special appreciation to Allen Tullos, my dear friend and editor of *Southern Spaces*. Also, many thanks to *Southern Spaces* staff members Stephanie Bryan, Madison Elkins, Amelia Golcheski, Camille Goldmon, Hannah Griggs, Rachel Kolb, Ra'Niqua Lee, and Sophia Leonard for their work on this piece. Thanks as well to Jon N. Hale for his suggestions. A special appreciation to Megan Slemons, GIS specialist with the Emory Center for Digital Scholarship, for assistance with maps and tables.

Overturning **Brown**

A New Era for 'School Choice' and Vouchers

The United States has never been closer to adopting a nationwide program in which the state and federal governments spend billions of tax dollars to finance largely unaccountable private schools to educate children from kindergarten through the twelfth grade. By the beginning of 2019, more than half of the fifty states had enacted a variety of voucher programs diverting public funds to private schools and in some places to home-schooling—often for the purported purpose of improving the education of low-income African American and Hispanic students. These programs use state appropriations or tax credits to divert public monies to support self-governing private schools, often with few requirements or restrictions.

The states have steadily enlarged these programs during recent decades as a result of persistent, intense lobbying from school choice advocates. Often, programs have started modestly with special-needs children, then expanded to a broader student population. School choice programs are spread across the nation, although the South has more than anywhere else.[1] In 2018, more than $2.1 billion dollars in state funds went to support private schooling—a sum larger than the annual state appropriation for public schools in any of thirteen states across the nation.[2]

In addition, there is growing support in Washington for establishing school choice nationwide. In his first address to a joint session of Congress, President Donald Trump declared:

Education is the civil rights issue of our time. (Applause.) I am calling upon members of both parties to pass an education bill that funds school choice for disadvantaged youth, including millions of African American and Latino children. (Applause.) These families should be free to choose the public, private, charter, magnet, religious, or home school that is right for them.[3]

During his campaign, Trump pledged that he would become the "nation's biggest cheerleader for school choice" and would provide states with the means to use $20 billion in federal money to create vouchers allowing children to attend the private schools of their choice. "There is no policy more in need of urgent change than our government-run education monopoly," he said, "[that] has trapped millions of African American and Hispanic youth" in failing schools.

Trump's secretary of education, Elizabeth "Betsy" DeVos, a wealthy donor to Republican causes and a leading advocate of public funding of religious private schools, stated in May 2017 that the Trump administration would propose "the most ambitious expansion of education choice in our nation's history" because the "cause is both right and just." The Trump administration proposed to divert more than $1 billion to private schools in the 2019 budget in order to fund "scholarships to students from low-income families that could be used to transfer to a private school." But DeVos has so far been unable to convince Congress to fund such programs directly.[4]

Support for federal funding of private schools is not a phenomenon only of the Trump administration. In 2012, the Republican candidate for president, Mitt Romney, issued an education "white paper" proposing public financing of tuition costs in private schools as the centerpiece of a new national education reform. The Romney

Over-Representation of White Students in Private Schools: 2012

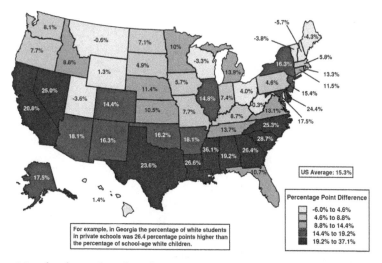

Map by the author, based on computations of National Center for Education Statistics data, 2012.

for President position paper proposed to overhaul the primary federal funding of K–12 public schools "so that low-income and special-needs students can choose which school to attend and bring their funding with them. The choices offered to students under this policy will include . . . private schools if permitted by state law."[5]

In 2014, U.S. senators Tim Scott of South Carolina and Lamar Alexander of Tennessee (ranking Republican on the committee for education) introduced legislation to enable federal funding for low-income and special-needs students in public schools to attend private schools. Alexander explained: "Allowing $2,100 federal scholarships to follow 11 million children to whatever school they attend would enable other school choice innovations, in the same way that developers rushed to provide applications for the iPhone platform."[6]

This momentum for vouchers found its way into the major federal tax overhaul enacted in 2017. Congress expanded the use of "529 savings plans" beyond paying for college costs so that tax-advantaged funds can now be used to pay up to $10,000 annually for costs of elementary and secondary education in K–12 private schools.[7] This change promises to become quite significant, especially for wealthier households. It opens up a fund—$328 billion and growing—from which monies can be diverted yearly to private K–12 schools.[8]

Sign protesting Betsy DeVos at a rally, Bellevue, Washington, October 13, 2017.

Civil Rights Rhetoric Echoes in 'School Choice' and Vouchers

"School choice" has no traditional or intrinsic meaning in the field of education, but over the last several decades it has become a political slogan for the claim that government should finance children's education from pre-kindergarten through the twelfth grade in schools outside the public system in order to provide parents with a choice. In recent years, charter schools have been included as a "school choice" option because many local districts and some states now authorize private profit-making or nonprofit entities to operate these schools independently, often without meeting requirements and rules that public schools must follow. In 2015, there were 2.8 million students in charter schools and 5.8 million students in private elementary and secondary schools across the United States.[9] This essay examines the history of government support for private schools as both the origin and primary foundation for the current movement for "school choice."

In claiming private "school choice" as right and just, President Trump and Secretary DeVos echo rhetoric that others have used to argue that publicly financed vouchers for children to attend private K–12 schools are a moral imperative. In articles such as "How School Choice Helps Advance Martin Luther King's Legacy," the Heritage Foundation has insisted that vouchers continue the civil rights movement. In 2011, the founder of the tax credit voucher program in Florida declared that school choice for low-income families "is one of the most important social justice issues of our time."[10]

One of Dr. King's children, in fact, joined the cause of vouchers for private schools in Florida to give "black, Latino, and Hispanic" children the same options as others. "This is about justice," Martin Luther King III stated in 2016. "This is about righteousness. This is about freedom—the freedom to choose for your family and your child."[11]

The political movement for "school choice" is employing the icons and language of civil rights and social justice to advance private school vouchers that fifty years ago were primary tools for segregationists to preserve unequal education for African American and Hispanic children. President Trump's call for a national program of "school choice" echoes the language of George Wallace and others who demanded the federal government and U.S. courts permit Alabama and the South to administer "freedom of choice" for elementary and secondary schools.

These apparent contradictions emerge from the unexamined legacy of segregationists who designed and developed effective, lasting strategies that frustrated and blocked K–12 school desegregation. It is a legacy that turns the icons and language of civil rights inside-out while thwarting the national goal of an effective, equitable system of education for all children.

Forgotten Segregationists

Historically, the methods and forms of segregation have been neither monolithic nor inert.[12] Southern segregationists held differing notions about the best ways to preserve school segregation along with their beliefs in racial superiority. As Sylvan Meyer observed in 1960, Southern segregationists included "all those whose views varied from a mild belief that the South would be better off maintaining as much racial separation as possible to those advocating insurrection rather than 'surrender' to any compromise whatsoever."[13] Many segregationist leaders who designed and implemented plans for school choice have been forgotten, as have their plethora of rationales, strategies, and tactics. They were never widely known, and popular culture has narrowed the cast to a small rogues' gallery.

Prevalent images include segregationists such as Alabama governor George Wallace, Birmingham police commissioner Eugene "Bull" Connor, and a bevy of other white leaders such as Mississippi senator James Eastland who endure as premiere political symbols—in large part because their defiant images in multiple confrontations with and condemnations of federal officials often were captured as television came of age in the 1960s.[14] A few, such as Wallace and North Carolina's Jesse Helms, remained on the national political stage for more than a decade.[15]

But George Wallace was only one type of segregationist—and hardly a representative figure for those more successful over time in frustrating and blocking school desegregation. Segregationists with other styles and backgrounds built the more lasting terms,

George C. Wallace, Eugene "Bull" Connor, James Eastland.

tools, and tactics that obstructed the Supreme Court's unanimous 1954 opinion in *Brown v. Board of Education*[16] outlawing segregated public education. This wider cast of white supremacists competed fiercely in shaping how and where segregated schools could be preserved. When political self-interest and racial ideology aligned, they occasionally cooperated. At times they shared a vocabulary against *Brown,* depicted as a federal edict to force the South to create "mixed schools," never to create equitable, desegregated or integrated schools.[17]

These white men included diehards, such as those found in the middle-class Citizens' Councils who usually pushed to abandon all public schooling rather than accept any desegregation. Some Citizens' Council leaders, however, came to recognize exceptions to absolute, complete segregation. Ku Klux Klanners, especially in the Deep South, were also dead-set against a single black child entering an all-white school and were willing to use extra-legal intimidation and violence. Others, such as South Carolina governor Jimmy Byrnes, believed that the impact of *Brown* could be postponed indefinitely or avoided in large measure by building new black schools so that separate schools appeared closer to equal.

Political leaders such as Georgia's Ernest Vandiver won office by campaigning on a slogan of "No, not one" African American child would ever be allowed in a white school but discovered after entering the governor's office that complete, absolute segregation was impossible to achieve—and counter-productive to preserving as many virtually segregated schools as possible. There were segregationists such as Alabama state senator Albert Boutwell—who later as a "moderate" mayoral candidate defeated "Bull" Connor—and Birmingham corporate attorney Forney Johnston. While Wallace began as a white liberal before shifting his politics so he could become governor, Boutwell and Johnston were the first segregationist leaders to develop a variety of strategies, tactics, and rationales for school choice that often delayed and defeated the promise of *Brown*.

Resistance to school desegregation differed across the states of the former Confederacy according to class, geography, religion, and political ambition.[18] Only by recovering and understanding the work of a wider cast of white actors who crafted enduring tools and strategies protecting segregation can the reactionary heritage of today's school choice become clear. As Justin Driver has found, the efforts of these segregationist leaders "to maintain white supremacy were often considerably more sophisticated, self-aware, and nuanced than the cartoonish depiction of Southern stupidity and hostility would admit."[19] These forgotten and ignored strategies help explain how today's proponents of public financing of private schools can employ the language of civil rights without widespread discredit. They also reveal how the origins and historical development of "freedom of choice" have shaped and continue to define the impact and role of "school choice" and vouchers in public education across the nation.[20]

School Choice and Vouchers Become Segregationist Tools

During the middle of the twentieth century, K–12 private schooling became intertwined with race and ethnicity as the Supreme Court issued opinions outlawing segregated graduate and professional public education.[21] These decisions had no impact on elementary and secondary public schools, but they signaled the direction the Court was moving.

From 1940 to 1950, private school enrollment in the South rose by more than 125,000 students—a 43-percent increase, and, for the first time since private enrollment numbers were documented, the rate of growth doubled that of the rest of the nation.

From 1950 to 1965, U.S. private school enrollment grew at unprecedented rates while the South's rate again exceeded the nation's. Whites in record numbers fled to traditional and newly formed private schools. From 1950 to 1958, the South's private school enrollment increased by more than 250,000 students. By 1965, there were nearly one million Southern private school students. Almost all were white.[22]

Legislatures passed laws authorizing vouchers and other means of transferring public assets and monies to private schools.[23] In November 1953, as it appeared the Supreme Court might strike down school segregation, white South Carolinians voted to repeal a section of their state constitution that provided for a "liberal system of free public schools"—to clear the way for establishing a private school system. Georgia became the first Southern state to pass a constitutional amendment enabling the legislature to send state, county, and municipal funds to "citizens of the State for educational purposes, in discharge of all obligation of the State to provide adequate education for its citizens." A month later, white Mississippians voted for a constitutional amendment granting the legislature power to close public schools and finance private ones. By the end of 1956, Virginia, Alabama, and North Carolina passed similar measures.[24]

From 1954 to 1965, Southern legislatures enacted as many as 450 laws and resolutions attempting to discredit, block, postpone, limit, or evade school desegregation. A large number of these acts allowed the re-direction of public resources, including school resources, to benefit private schools.[25] In 1956, the Georgia legislature permitted the leasing of public property to segregated private schools. Five years later, the state enacted a law to provide

African American elementary school students in class, Sylvania, Georgia, 1951.

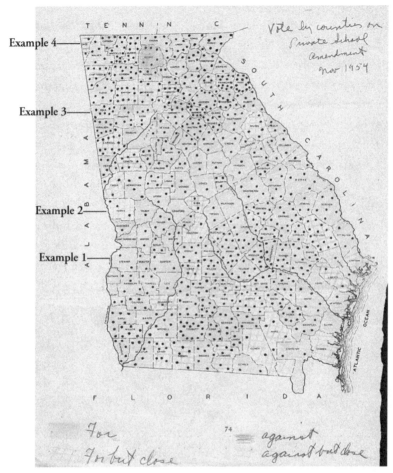

Vote by counties on private school amendment, Georgia, November 1954. Map by unknown creator. Shades are hard to distinguish in this black and white reproduction, but according to the map's key, shaded blue (Example 1) signifies "For," checkered blue (Example 2) signifies "For but close," shaded pink (Example 3) signifies "Against," and checkered pink (Example 4) signifies "Against but close."

vouchers for students to attend any nonsectarian private school, boldly declaring the act was to advance "the constitutional rights of school children to attend private schools of their choice in lieu of public schools."[26]

The North Carolina legislature enacted eight bills, the first of which was a constitutional amendment to authorize vouchers for private education and to allow whites to close public schools through a local referendum. In Alabama, Louisiana, Mississippi, and South Carolina, legislatures passed laws to publicly fund vouchers for private schools and to transfer public school property to private educational organizations. Citizens' Councils were active in setting up private schools, especially in Mississippi. The Virginia legislature declared its support for this "freedom of choice" movement by enacting a system of vouchers for private organizations and citizens.[27]

In addition to direct transfers of public funds and assets, some states employed tax schemes, including tax credits, to build and finance private school systems. In the Little Rock Crisis of 1957, after President Dwight Eisenhower was forced to call out federal troops to protect a handful of black children attempting to attend Central High School, Governor Orval Faubus funneled public monies through contracts and tax credits to the Little Rock Private School Corporation until the federal courts stopped the subterfuge (along with further attempts by Arkansas to enact vouchers). In 1959, Georgia governor Ernest Vandiver led the legislature in passing the six segregation bills, including one that supported "the establishment of bona fide private schools by allowing taxpayers credits upon their State income tax returns for contributions to such institutions."[28]

In the same year, Florida governor LeRoy Collins successfully opposed a legislative initiative to pass a constitutional amendment to allow state tax credits for private school contributions. In Prince Edward County and other locations in Virginia, officials used both direct payments and tax credits to build private schools until the

Students being educated via television while the schools were closed to avoid desegregation, Little Rock, Arkansas, September 1958. Photographs by Thomas J. O'Halloran.

Child watching a march protesting the admission of "Little Rock Nine" to Central High School, Little Rock, Arkansas, August 20, 1959. Photograph by John T. Bledsoe.

federal courts halted both. In Mississippi, after federal courts struck down a direct tuition grant to private schools, Governor John Bell Williams proposed a state tax credit as he searched for the "ways and means of rendering assistance" for white flight to private schools.[29]

By 1965, seven states had enacted some type of voucher that enabled the largest growth of private schools in the South's history. Yet, vouchers as a preferred and essential method of resistance to *Brown* did not stand alone but worked most effectively through larger plans that emerged from the different states. These plans were not uniform, but most incorporated strategies and language that have evolved and endured as the ways and means by which vouchers, school choice, and private schooling have escaped the stigma of their segregationist origins without losing much of the same purpose or effect.

Preserving Virtual School Segregation through Vouchers

During the era of massive resistance, several state legislatures and governors established committees or commissions to develop options for preserving segregation. These strategy groups were often known by the name of the persons chairing them—usually a senior legislator or well-known businessman. In Alabama, it was the Boutwell Committee, led by a prominent, well-to-do state senator. In South Carolina, a wealthy state senator chaired the Gressette Committee. The Pearsall Committee in North Carolina was named for its businessman leader; an Atlanta business leader guided Georgia's Sibley Commission. In Virginia, both of its strategy commissions were named for their prominent businessmen chairs.

The strategy groups issued recommendations in written reports explaining the imperatives for segregation, the rationale for preserving it, including arguments for why segregation was advantageous to black families, and the different tactics of resistance. These reports demonstrate that segregationist leaders came to understand that vouchers and other forms of aid to private schools worked best in conjunction with a variety of other tactics and strategies for defeating *Brown*.

ALABAMA: "BIG MULES" DEVELOP A FREEDOM OF CHOICE PLAN

In October 1954, barely five months after *Brown*, the Boutwell Committee became the first strategy group to lay out a complete, multifaceted plan of resistance. As a moderate segregationist, state senator Albert Boutwell did not believe it feasible or advisable to maintain old segregation laws and disavowed the use of force.[30] Perhaps the Boutwell plan's chief architect and certainly its primary intellectual force was Forney Johnston, a brilliant segregationist and corporate attorney in Birmingham who represented Alabama's "Big Mules"—coal companies, railroads, and wealthy industrialists and investors who profited from Birmingham's exploitative heavy industries. As a backroom politician and former governor's son, Johnston adroitly maneuvered in politics and law to protect the corporate interests he represented and to preserve his notion of segregation. He had managed a 1924 presidential campaign, mounted major legal challenges to New Deal economic reforms, and worked behind the scenes to secure pardons for the "Scottsboro

Front page of newspaper published by the Citizens' Council in Jackson, Mississippi, November 1955.

Boys"—but only to prevent growing national support for federal intervention in "states' rights."[31]

The Boutwell report decried "forced integration," claiming it would lead to "violence, disorder, and tension for the state and its children." It warned that if the federal courts pursued "coerced integration," white employers would fire black employees involved in such efforts and the federal courts would prompt inevitable violence among "the least stable and least mentally matured and responsible members of both races." The report also suggested that "compulsory integration" would devastate public school finances by estranging "white people, who pay by far the greater part of taxes which maintain the schools."

The Boutwell plan sought to assure two goals ("Education for all children of the state" and "No compulsory mixing of races in our schools") by proposing four basic strategies:

- Eliminate any "prohibition against the operation of mixed schools, attended by both races" in the current state constitution and laws. In other words, Alabama laws would "concede the right of white and negro families to send their children to mixed public schools." This change would enshrine "the principle of freedom of choice" to enable parents to select the school their children should attend—within certain predetermined conditions and qualifications.

- Remove any suggestion from the state constitution that there is a right of education or an obligation of the state to fund public schoolchildren and establish a "policy of the State of Alabama to foster and promote the education of its citizens *in a manner and extent consistent with its available resources, and the willingness and ability of the individual student* [emphasis added]."

- Invest the legislature with constitutional powers to enable local school officials to determine the conditions and qualifications for "eligibility, admission, and allocation of pupils, including the power to refuse admission to individuals or groups whose deficiencies in scholastic aptitude would compel undue lowering of school standards.

• Grant the legislature the constitutional power to provide vouchers and other tax funds in "support and furtherance of education in other ways than the operation of public schools" for both black and white children.[32]

In effect, the plan would establish in the name of school "choice" a three-school system, instead of a dual school system. The new system would enable children to attend all-white schools, all-black schools, or desegregated schools in a state-financed system of public and private schools.

With only one "nay" vote, the legislature passed the proposals to revise the state constitution, and white voters of Alabama ratified the amendments in 1956 to set up the plan's framework. Alabama's Citizens' Council (called "manicured Kluxism" by the editor of the *Montgomery Advertiser*) worried that the proposals were weak. The Council's leader, state senator Sam Engelhardt, had earlier proposed legislation to close all public schools and use vouchers for white parents to enroll in private schools in order to "keep every brick in our segregation wall intact." Alabama governor James E. "Big Jim" Folsom opposed all of these measures. "I wouldn't want to sign a bill that would let rich folks send their kids all to one school and the poor folks to another school," the populist Folsom declared.[33]

While the constitutional amendments recommended by the Boutwell Committee were pending before the legislature, Forney Johnston gave a speech to the Alabama Bar Association that identified the plan's legal underpinnings: "the liberty of parents to direct the basic conditions under which their children shall be educated." Quoting from the 1925 U.S. Supreme Court opinion that struck down an Oregon statute requiring all disability-free children to attend a public school,[34] Johnston declared: "This parental liberty, like other liberties, is not absolute; but is limited only by an overriding necessity for community order or welfare, reflected not in some remote Federal pronouncement, but in the grass-root exercise of state police power, by the State acting in its sovereign capacity."

Johnston argued that the Boutwell plan provided freedom of choice without regard to race and, in that context, the federal courts could not require white parents to send their children to a desegregated school, although some white parents could decide to do so. "If the 14th Amendment now says that a state cannot inhibit the freedom of negroes to attend schools with white people, what does it say about the freedom of white people to choose not to go to school with negroes?" Johnston answered his own question. Virtually segregated schools could continue through this freedom of choice in a new system of education where the government financed both public and private schools, where there was "ordinary and customary geographical districting" for public schools, and where the independent "application of accepted educational tests and standards" by both private and public schools were the terms for admitting students.

This type of school system would permit parental choice for a desegregated school, all-white school, or all-black school within a structure and standards that were expressly nonracial. "If the members of a race are thereby deprived of access to a school attended by the other race," Johnston observed, "the result is attributable

James "Big Jim" Folsom campaigning for governor, Mobile, Alabama, June 6, 1946.

not to compulsion by the state but to the inconsistent choices of free citizens. Under such circumstances, the state is obliged to give effect to the desire of parents without compulsion against either side."[35]

The full details of the Boutwell plan failed to become law in 1955 in large measure because of the direct and behind-the-scenes opposition of Governor Folsom, who downplayed the *Brown* decision and on many other issues fought with Black Belt politicians and Birmingham's "Big Mules" and their lawyers such as Johnston. Folsom also vetoed a handful of local bills that attempted to punish black teachers if they voiced support for desegregation, but the legislature passed the segregationists' pupil placement bill by a veto-proof margin.

The new pupil placement law for public schools was sponsored by Senator Sam Engelhardt, the Citizens' Council leader who had come to embrace the Boutwell Committee's concepts and strategies.

The law asserted it had nothing to do with segregation, but aimed to advance each child's education:

> To establish a practical school system whereby the state's school program can be adapted to each pupil's ability to learn. To this end it provides a modern school placement system, so that pupils can be so grouped that the less advanced pupils shall not be penalized by being placed in the class with pupils who are more advanced or capable of learning at a more rapid rate, and conversely, that exceptionally bright and able pupils shall not be held back to a level below their ability to learn.

The law empowered local school boards alone to make decisions about which school each student was assigned to attend based on the following factors: tests of student aptitude and ability as well as the distance of school from a pupil's home; a pupil's educational background and home environment; a student's long-established ties of friendship or the dangers of placing a pupil in hostile surroundings absent former friends and "associates"; a pupil's own wishes as evidenced by a written request from his parents or guardian to be assigned to a particular school; and whether, in the judgment of the school board, the assignment would cause or tend to cause a breach of the peace, riot, or "affray." The law provided for a complicated, costly appeal process, if parents disagreed with the board's decision. Not one word in the legislation mentioned segregation, integration, or a child's race.[36]

A year later, with the Montgomery bus boycott threatening to end segregated seating in the state capital, the federal courts ordered the admission of Autherine Lucy, a black woman, into the University of Alabama, and white-led race riots broke out in Tuscaloosa.[37]

Autherine Lucy and her lawyers, Thurgood Marshall, Arthur Shores, and Constance Baker Motley, walking past the federal courthouse on the day a judge ordered her readmission to the University of Alabama, Birmingham, Alabama, February 29, 1956. Photograph by Norman Dean.

Afterwards, the legislature decided it was time to place before voters the basic parts of the Boutwell plan or, as it was publicly called, the "Freedom of Choice Plan." Folsom declared the legislation "hogwash" and many of his supporters opposed it. It also was opposed by diehards such as Asa Carter, a Citizens' Council (and soon Klan) leader, since the proposal removed all constitutional requirements for the complete separation of the races in the schools.

Alabama's virtually all-white electorate approved the "freedom of choice" amendments to the constitution with 61 percent of the vote, and the Boutwell plan's key elements became the operating terms for the strategy to resist and slow school desegregation in the Heart of Dixie.

John Patterson won the race for governor in 1958 as a hard-edged, proven segregationist who, as Alabama attorney general, had attempted to put the NAACP out of business through a series of persistent, harassing lawsuits—an attack commenced after a strategy meeting that included Forney Johnston. As governor, Patterson assured white Alabamians that "I would not agree under any circumstances to operate an integrated school," but, with Boutwell serving as lieutenant governor, he followed the spirit and letter of the Boutwell-Johnston strategy. It proved remarkably successful. During Patterson's four years in the governor's mansion, the U.S. Supreme Court upheld Alabama's pupil placement law on its face as constitutional and, as Patterson later boasted, no Alabama public school was ever desegregated while he was governor.[38]

Alabama's approach to controlling school desegregation changed dramatically in 1963 after George Wallace won the race for governor by making good on his promise—uttered after losing to Patterson in 1958—that "no other son-of-a-bitch will ever out-nigger me again."[39] Wallace defeated Folsom, Boutwell, and "Bull" Connor, among others. In his inaugural speech written by Asa Carter, Wallace proclaimed words that have resounded across the decades:

> Today I have stood, where once Jefferson Davis stood. . . . Let us . . . send our answer to the tyranny that clanks its chains upon the South. . . . I draw the line in the dust and toss the gauntlet before the feet of tyranny . . . and I say . . . segregation now . . . segregation tomorrow . . . segregation forever.[40]

Governor Wallace kicked off an orchestrated, theatrical performance of massive resistance a few months later when he stood in the schoolhouse door to decry federal encroachment on state

WSB-TV newsfilm clip of Alabama governor George C. Wallace blocking the doorway of the University of Alabama, June 11, 1963.

sovereignty and to protest the admission of two black students to the University of Alabama, which had a total enrollment of almost ten thousand students. Afterwards, Wallace led the state government in replaying strategies used earlier in Mississippi and Louisiana, including the formation of state spy commissions to monitor and intimidate civil right activists. His administration coordinated with the Klan and the Citizens' Council, and Wallace's frequent public pronouncements left little doubt that Alabama's school program had nothing to do with the Boutwell Committee's earlier stated purposes of advancing "each pupil's ability to learn" and everything to do with preserving absolute segregation.

Buoyed by national news coverage and by the enthusiastic support of white Alabamians that came as a result of Jim Crow grandstanding, Wallace had no intention of permitting any Alabama official to accept or implement token integration in the schools without an opportunity for him to publicly display his fight for complete segregation. The governor called out state troopers to surround school buildings in several Alabama towns—even when local white school boards had decided to permit a small number of black children to cross the color line.

In response, civil rights attorneys returned to federal court with

Above: State troopers preventing Henry Hobdy and Dorothy Davis from entering Murphy High School, Mobile, Alabama, September 9, 1963. Right: Segregationist rhetoric inspired crowds of white protesters, like these in Birmingham in October 1963, outside schools across Alabama.

Birmingham Demonstrators
Schools were boycotted.

new evidence from Wallace's statements and actions that the school laws and their enforcement were intended to block *Brown*, and the courts began striking down the state's education laws—including its private school voucher law—and ordering school desegregation. As his lawyers lost in the federal courts, Wallace kept racial politics center stage, creating an environment for violence and capturing the adulation of the white diehards. He also attracted the nation's attention by expanding and amplifying the provocative rhetoric of total, massive federal resistance. Wallace became in the political imaginary one of the nation's enduring Southern segregationist icons.[41]

The Other Southern States: "Freedom from Compulsory Association" by Any or Many Means

Six other states—Mississippi, Louisiana, Virginia, North Carolina, South Carolina, and Georgia—also created strategy groups to block school desegregation. Each group had its own distinct design and role within the dynamics of how each state built massive resistance to *Brown,* but most shared similar characteristics and tactics. All adopted vouchers for private schools.

In Mississippi, white voters approved state constitutional changes recommended by Governor Hugh White's advisory group that authorized state funding for children to attend their parents' choice of a private school and for transferring public school properties to private schools. Afterwards, the strategy committee did little more since Mississippi's white leaders employed other groups and strategies as their first line of defense. The legislature approved small funding increases for black public schools in an attempt to convince black citizens that the state would move closer to "separate but equal" facilities.

for segregated private schools in Surry County, Virginia, and in the state of Alabama. Georgia has practically given up its tuition grant program. Can Mississippi afford to experiment with an expensive program of doubtful constitutionality?

DON'T LET IT HAPPEN HERE!

The tuition grant system is not the only threat to our public schools. In Mississippi there are some short-sighted persons who advocate abandoning the schools and may resort to thoughtless acts in order to close or destroy them. We know that such people represent an insignificant number of our citizens. But they are extremely vocal. We have only to look back at Little Rock, New Orleans and Clinton, Tenn. to see the tragic result of this kind of influence. It could lead to violence, to helmeted troops with fixed bayonets on our school grounds, to scars on our political, social and business life which can never be removed.

WHAT WE CAN DO

To responsible Mississippians, the slow erosion of our schools through impractical schemes like tuition grants would be a tragic waste. Closing our schools is unthinkable. Violence, or occupation by federal troops, would be catastrophic.

We must therefore protect our public school system from internal dissolution and outside interference. Some few will turn their backs on this responsibility. Others will wring their hands ineffectually. But thoughtful citizens will realize that we must all work together to protect our children's heritage by:

1. Giving our support to school authorities and other public officials who have been given orders by The Courts which they must obey and are working to make this transition a peaceful one.

2. Working to create a community climate in which law and order are respected and in which violence and lawlessness are unacceptable.

3. Making the facts about the pitfalls of the tuition grant system known to every parent, to every taxpayer.

4. Continuing to upgrade our public schools by securing higher standards, bet-

ter teachers pay, and community-wide interest in the schools.

MISSISSIPPIANS FOR PUBLIC EDUCATION

The principles stated above are the goals of Mississippians for Public Education. Ours is a statewide, non-profit, independent organization.

We have faith in our fellow Mississippians and know that they want law and order. We believe that when they know the facts about our schools, they will work together to protect them. To give the widest circulation to these facts is a basic part of our program.

As parents, taxpayers and citizens, we are pledged to create the kind of community climate in which public education can flourish and grow in an atmosphere of good will and within the framework of the law. We are not a forum for debating the pros and cons of desegregation or state's rights or any political question. Our goal is solely to protect, preserve and promote our public school system.

We invite all responsible Mississippians to join with us in attaining this goal. Simply fill out the coupon below.

Pres. ..... MRS. GORDON HENDERSON
Jackson
1st. V. Pres. .... MRS. MARGE CURET
Biloxi
2nd V. Pres. ..... MRS. JACK REED
Tupelo
Secty. .. MRS. KENNETH HAXTON, JR.
Greenville
Treas. .... MRS. THOMAS WARD
Meridian

To: Mississippians For Public Education
P. O. Box 2294
Jackson, Miss., 39205

Yes I would like to support Public Education in Mississippi. Enclosed is my $2.00*

or $..........

Name ....

Address ....

City .... Zone ....

*Minimum; more will help send this information to other homes.

A TIME TO SPEAK...

MISSISSIPPIANS FOR PUBLIC EDUCATION

A pamphlet distributed by Mississippians for Public Education, Jackson, Mississippi.

What sort of education do we want for our children? Most parents would answer this question as ours. We want to give them:

—A calm educational atmosphere where they can learn, without fear of violence and unrest.

—A high quality curriculum to develop their minds, and their physical well-being for job preparation and good citizenship.

—The best teachers available.

—School buildings with high standards of sanitation, equipped with lab facilities, teaching aids, libraries and athletic equipment.

These are natural, normal goals. As parents, we have an obligation to work for their accomplishment. As taxpayers, we have a duty to see them achieved with thrift and good management. As citizens, we have a right to ask that our schools be protected from any impractical plan that would endanger their future development.

But all of these goals are seriously threatened today. In answer to court orders to desegregate schools in September, 1964, some voices demand implementation of a tuition grant system which would enable parents to send their children to private schools paid for by a state grant of $185 per pupil.

Let us examine this idea on its past performance — without heat or rancor — to see what it would mean for our children, for our school system, and for the economy of our state.

WHAT HARM TO OUR CHILDREN?

There is no existing private school system in Mississippi which could absorb a massive influx of tuition grant students. Tuition grant schools would therefore have to be hastily organized in unused or abandoned buildings, garages, private homes. The state can make no provisions for buildings, books, transportation, lab facilities or athletic equipment. There would be no guarantee of such fundamentals as good sanitation and regular maintenance. The supervision of uniform standards by public school officials are two of the most valuable assets of our state public school system. These would not be available under the tuition grant plan. Also,

the state might give accreditation to the tuition grant schools, but students graduating from them might have difficulty in gaining admission to first-rate colleges outside the state.

These predictions are not idle speculation. They are based on the actual experience of schools in other Southern states. As reported by the Public Affairs Research Council of Louisiana, Inc., in October, 1963, here is one example of a school in which 100% of the student's attending in 1962-63 received tuition grants. This school "located in Lake Charles, was opened in 1960, and at the beginning of the present school year had an enrollment of 50 students." This institution offers instruction in grades 1 through 12. For the current school year it is employing a total of five teachers, three of whom do not have a college degree. The principal is one of the five teachers and is also one of those who has not finished college. This institution has neither a library nor a laboratory."

WHAT COST TO OUR TAXPAYERS?

The cost to the Louisiana taxpayer during the 1963-64 school year was estimated at $3,600,000, to be paid by sales tax receipts diverted from the general welfare fund. In Virginia, taxpayers paid $2,253,000 for their tuition grant system in 1962-63.

Ironically, a sizeable portion of these tax dollars has been expended on children already in private schools. In Louisiana, 40% of the money went to people whose children were in private schools. Similarly, in Georgia, 80% of the applicants were parents with children already enrolled in private schools.

Plans in Mississippi could mean a tax bill many times that of Louisiana or Virginia. Any money spent for tuition grants for the school year 1964-65 will be in addition to the money already allocated for public schools. Tuition grant money cannot be taken from public school funds. The allocated public school money will be spent on the public schools as already planned. When we remember that our state has the lowest per capita income of any in the fifty states, we realize that the additional tax

burden could spell serious financial trouble for many individuals and businesses.

WHAT DANGER TO OUR SCHOOLS?

Private schools have always had a place in American education, but every community needs a strong public school system. Shifting a sizeable number of students from public schools to tuition grant private schools could undermine our public school system.

—In a state where teacher's salaries are the lowest in the country, it has been a serious problem to increase teacher's benefits. Under the tuition grant system many teachers now employed in the public schools might be out of their jobs and state retirement would not be available to them. New teachers would certainly not be attracted to teach in the state.

—Empty school buildings are a magnet for vandals and arsonists. For example, in Dublin, Georgia, an abandoned white school erected in 1957 for $350,000 has been gutted by vandals. It is now unusable.

—In Mississippi, use of the tuition grant system could mean the slow starvation of our public schools. Our state school budget is based on the Average Daily Attendance Law. If tuition grants are widely used, the Average Daily Attendance will shrink correspondingly, and with it, the funds allocated to the schools for the following year. This means that should the tuition grant system end, children returning to public schools might find that insufficient money has been allocated for teachers, equipment and books had been allocated.

IMPRACTICAL, UNECONOMIC AND ... ILLEGAL

Tuition grant programs have been instituted to circumvent desegregation of public schools. However, in Virginia and Louisiana where they have been most extensively used they have not preserved segregation. The number of children in desegregated schools has increased every year. Furthermore, the issuing of grants for use in segregated schools in Virginia, Louisiana and Alabama is being challenged in the courts. Federal judges have already prohibited the use of such grants

Mississippi's primary strategies to block school desegregation involved private and public agencies that undertook economic and social intimidation, behind-the-scenes spying, physical threats, and violence. The Mississippi Sovereignty Commission kept tabs on "agitators" in conjunction with the Citizens' Council, the Klan, and other vigilante groups.[42]

Other states used legal and extra-legal tactics to keep schools segregated, but, as one author wrote, "Mississippi verged on totalitarianism."[43] "This is a fight for white supremacy," declared the editor of the *Jackson Daily News*, returning to public language often abandoned by segregationists elsewhere. "[T]here will be no room for neutrals or non-combatants." Local black leaders such as Leake County sisters Winson and Dovie Hudson faced combatants

1956 NAACP recruitment poster displayed by, from left, Henry L. Moon, director of public relations; Roy Wilkins, executive secretary; Herbert Hill, labor secretary, and Thurgood Marshall, special counsel.

as they continued to challenge school segregation, despite economic reprisals, physical threats, and more than one bombing of their own homes. "I'm going to stay here and pay the cost, no matter what it is," Dovie Hudson assured Mississippi NAACP field secretary Medgar Evers, who soon afterwards was murdered in his own driveway in Jackson. Anyone connected to school desegregation or civil rights work in Mississippi ran a real risk of being fired from work, thrown out of their house, beaten, bombed, or shot at. Several were killed.[44]

As a result, school desegregation moved very slowly in Mississippi. In 1969, fifteen years after *Brown*, the U.S. Supreme Court found that Mississippi had made hardly any strides in undoing "segregated conditions" and ordered every school district in the state "to terminate dual school systems at once." Aided by Citizens' Council chapters, segregation academies sprung up across the state, and Mississippi's public schools desegregated only when and where civil rights lawyers won their day in federal courts.[45]

The strategy group in Louisiana was headed by long-time state senator William M. Rainach, who also spearheaded the creation of Louisiana's Citizens' Councils.[46] The Rainach Committee became a coordinating agency as much for action as for legislative strategy. It helped to mount legal roadblocks to school desegregation, orchestrated legal attacks on black activist organizations, and spurred efforts to remove or block black voting in close collaboration with the Louisiana Sovereignty Commission. Like many other state agencies across the South, the committee condemned integration as the work of communists.

Following the Rainach Committee's recommendations, the legislature in 1958 authorized public schools to become private education cooperatives and a voucher program for white students to attend nonreligious private schools.[47] Local NAACP leader Daniel

WSB-TV newsfilm clip of an interracial classroom, New Orleans, Louisiana, December 1, 1960.

Boyd suggested to national legal director Thurgood Marshall that "the Luzanna legislature will keep ignoring any and all court decisions until a number of them are jailed."[48] In 1960, refusing further delays, U.S. District Judge Skelly Wright ordered the desegregation of New Orleans's 9th Ward elementary school.

Amid death threats, a six-year-old black girl, Ruby Bridges, entered the previously all-white school with an escort of federal marshals protecting her from a mob of angry, screaming white men and women. Senator Rainach abandoned his role as strategist in order to appear publicly more attractive as he campaigned to become governor. "Let's use the 'scorched earth policy,'" he proclaimed at a Citizens' Council rally.

Jimmie Davis became the newly elected governor and quickly disbanded Rainach's committee. Following other Southern governors, Davis pushed the legislature to revoke all overt segregation laws and pass race-neutral programs for advancing freedom of choice for parents. A new voucher law also made no mention of race; it allowed any Louisiana child eligible to receive a state-funded voucher to attend a nonprofit, nonsectarian private school.[49]

The race-neutral program began in 1962, operated for four years, and distributed more than fifty-five thousand vouchers. The

Top, U.S. marshals escort Ruby Bridges at William Frantz Elementary School, New Orleans, Louisiana, November 14, 1960. Bottom, Bridges and President Barack Obama discussing Norman Rockwell's "The Problem We All Live With" painting, in the White House, 2011.

vast majority of state funds went to the families of white students, although existing records show that about 7 percent of all vouchers supported students from black families. All voucher-supported private schools were segregated by race—either all-white or all-black.

After the voucher law was challenged in federal court, four all-black private schools joined the state government in defending the program. The legislature renamed its voucher commission the "Louisiana Education Commission for Needy Children" with the professed purpose of addressing the problems of juvenile delinquency and school dropouts as well as the special needs of "retarded children" as it declared "that the parent, not the State of Louisiana, shall be the determining force which shall decide on the type of education ultimately received by the child." A federal court panel, however, found the "necessary effect of the Louisiana tuition grants [was] to establish . . . a system of segregated schools for white children, in violation of the equal protection clause."[50]

Thomas J. Pearsall, a North Carolina attorney, businessman, and former speaker of the state House of Representatives, chaired the North Carolina strategy committee responsible for finding a response to *Brown*. The Pearsall Committee originally had three African Americans among twenty members. Its first report proposed only a pupil assignment act mirroring the basics of Alabama's law. It empowered local school officials to assign students according to factors such as community relations, student ability, school capacity, and geographic location—without any mention of race.[51]

Hardline segregationists such as future U.S. Senator Jesse Helms dismissed the report, arguing that the state had to choose between "integrated public schools and free choice private schools." North Carolina attorney general Beverly Lake, also later a U.S. senator, made the same argument urging the closure of public schools and the provision of vouchers for white children to attend totally segregated private schools.[52]

In a second report in April 1956, the now all-white Pearsall Committee declared that it would "preserve a segregated system" like the one in the past and suggested ways to move from a "segregated-by-law system" to a segregated-by-choice system. The report reminded local school officials that, due to the U.S. Supreme Court, there can be "no racial segregation by law," but nothing prohibited them from making "assignment according to natural racial preference and the administrative determination of

First-grade class of African American and white school children at Albemarle Road Elementary School, Charlotte, North Carolina, February 21, 1973. Photograph by Warren K. Leffler.

what is best for the child." It recommended vouchers wherever "a child cannot be conveniently assigned to a non-mixed public school," regardless of the child's race, so long as the child's parent did not want a desegregated school. The committee insisted that while the Supreme Court had struck down laws "compelling the separation of the races in public schools," no court could compel "the mixing of the races."

Over the next decade, most North Carolina schools slowly admitted a token number of black students in previously all-white schools, although many small, rural school districts in eastern North Carolina resisted until a court order required the admission of a token number of black children in previously all-white schools. The Pearsall Plan began to crumble when North Carolina civil rights attorney Julius Chambers persuaded a federal three-judge panel in

1966 that "the payment of tuition grants is clearly state action, and unquestionably impermissible." A year earlier, Chambers's home had been bombed twice and his car firebombed once as a result of his willingness to openly challenge school segregation. Following his own advice to others— "Keep fighting"—Chambers convinced the federal court that the "state may not circumvent the Constitution by giving financial encouragement to individuals to follow a course which defeats desegregation."[53]

In Virginia, there were two strategy commissions. The first was chaired by businessman and state senator Garland Gray. In November 1955, it recommended the three basic methods of resistance first outlined by Alabama's Boutwell Committee: 1) investing local school officials with broad discretion to assign public school students on the basis of apparently non-racial factors such as availability of facilities and transportation, health, and aptitude of the child; 2) authorizing vouchers and other payments to private schools; and 3) permitting parents, without regard to race, to receive state-funded vouchers to attend private schools if their children were assigned to desegregated schools.

The Gray Commission's proposals implied that it would preserve only virtual segregation, not total segregation—an approach that many Virginia politicians defiantly opposed.[54] Bowing to the hardline segregationists, state leaders rejected the Gray Commission's recommendation in favor of massive resistance. The legislature declared desegregation a "clear and present danger" that required closing public schools when necessary. The new law also discarded the Gray Commission's recommendation to give local school boards the authority to make pupil assignments on terms without expressly mentioning race. The state board of education was specifically authorized to prevent assigning white and black

Two Governors Commemorate Civil War
Dressed in period costumes at Montgomery celebration: Alabama Gov. John Patterson, left, and Virginia Gov. J. Lindsay Almond Jr.

Newspaper clipping from Southern School News, *Nashville, Tennessee, March 1961, of Alabama and Virginia governors, in Montgomery, celebrating centennial of the start of the Civil War.*

students in the same school.[55]

Lindsay Almond became Virginia's new governor in 1957 after a campaign in which he supported the hardline approach. "I'd rather lose my right arm," he proclaimed, "than to see one nigra child enter the white schools of Virginia." But, once in office, Governor Almond was persuaded by business leaders and others to establish a second commission, named after its chair, state senator Mosby

Perrow, a prosperous lawyer and farmer. The Perrow Commission's report echoed the Gray Commission's "twin principles of local determination and *freedom of choice.*" It also recommended adopting the strategies of the earlier Gray Commission and Alabama's Boutwell Committee: abandon any mention of race; allow local, flexible pupil placement on factors without explicit mention of race; create vouchers or so-called "scholarships."

The Perrow report did not specify exact terms for proposed legislation in each area since its members were not certain at that moment if a "three school plan," first envisioned in Alabama five years earlier, would be successfully defended in the courts. It did recommend a new uniform testing program—but testing only for the public schools, not for the private schools supported by vouchers.[56]

Not all local jurisdictions followed the Perrow report. Some, such as Prince Edward County, maintained absolute segregation by closing the county's public schools and providing county tax credit scholarships to supplement state vouchers for white children to attend private schools. In 1964, however, Justice Hugo Black issued the Supreme Court opinion outlawing the diehard segregationists' schemes. The Court ordered the public schools reopened on a desegregated basis and held that both tax credit and direct vouchers were unconstitutional.[57]

Senator Marion Gressette, chair of the South Carolina Segregation School Committee—first created by Governor Jimmy Byrnes and the state legislature in 1951—led resistance to court-ordered desegregation for more than twenty years. The Gressette Committee believed the best defense against the federal courts was to move "with caution and with a minimum of publicity" and to report publicly as little as possible.[58]

Before *Brown*, Governor Byrnes initiated an aggressive state-wide building program of segregated schools for black children to bolster the legal argument that "separate but equal" was equal and constitutional, but the passage of a state constitutional amendment two years before *Brown* also permitted South Carolina to close its public schools—a clear message to the black population to leave segregation as it had been.

After *Brown*, Byrnes suspended the black school construction program, but restarted it once persuaded by the Gressette Committee that the program remained a useful incentive for black parents to keep their children in segregated, all-black schools instead of seeking admission to all-white public schools.[59]

Following the Gressette Committee's recommendations, the legislature also passed a pupil assignment bill giving local school boards the authority to make all decisions about attendance based on a family's geographic location and a child's scholastic aptitude (e.g., "each child shall be considered individually") without mention of race. Gressette understood that this color-blind standard in pupil placement could be a barrier to widespread school desegregation because of residential segregation. As the staff director of the Gressette Committee privately observed, local school boards could also decide, even where housing segregation did not preserve separate schools, that "there are few Negroes educationally qualified to go to schools with similarly aged white children."[60]

The president of the South Carolina Farm Bureau echoed the analysis made earlier by Alabama corporate attorney Forney Johnston when he observed: "If Negroes are to have the right of free choice in attending separate or mixed schools if they wish, then even the Supreme Court cannot deny to white people that same free choice of sending their children to separate or mixed schools."[61]

The state's acceptance of token desegregation in order to keep schools virtually segregated did not satisfy South Carolina's hard-liners, but the Gressette Committee's approach prevailed even as escalating racial violence and state-sponsored intimidation against black and white activists, especially the NAACP, continued.[62] Over time, and without mentioning race, the South Carolina legislature repealed compulsory attendance in public schools, pushed decision-making about school enrollment and school closing to local districts, permitted white students living in racially diverse areas to transfer to a nearby virtually segregated school district, and established tax exemptions for children attending private schools.[63]

On January 28, 1963, following a federal court order, Harvey Gantt became the first African American since Reconstruction to enroll in a state university in South Carolina when he was admitted to Clemson without incident. Gantt had attended college in Iowa but decided: "I was homesick for the South, I was a child of the South, and that's where I wanted to go."[64]

The next day, South Carolina's new governor, Donald Russell, announced that the state would provide parents with vouchers or "scholarship grants" to send their children to nonsectarian private schools. Russell did not mention race. He argued that vouchers

WSB-TV newsfilm clip of Harvey Gantt enrolling at Clemson University, Clemson, South Carolina, January 2, 1963.

would require public schools to compete with private ones for students and "this competition would stimulate progress in public education." The Gressette Committee reported that vouchers would "offer to all our citizens the broadest possible freedom of choice."[65]

In May 1968, after hearing arguments on the voucher program from Matthew Perry and Ernest Finney Jr. (two African American attorneys who later became judges), a panel of three federal judges declared the "purpose, motive and effect of the Act is to unconstitutionally circumvent the requirement . . . that the State of South Carolina not discriminate on the basis of race or color in its public educational system."[66]

In Georgia in 1950, more than two hundred African American students and parents filed a lawsuit claiming unequal education on account of race and seeking admission to all-white schools in Atlanta. Governor Herman Talmadge warned, "Our rifles are ready" to resist any court desegregation order. Roy Harris, an influential political operative and future head of the Citizens' Council, called for the closure of the state's public schools and the creation of a tax-funded private school system.[67]

Over the next few years, the General Assembly passed laws cutting off funding to any public school that a federal court ordered to desegregate. It also passed laws increasing school funding for segregated black schools and, after *Brown* was argued in 1953, additional laws enabled white voters to approve a constitutional amendment to permit vouchers for private schooling. Georgia's attorney general, Eugene Cook, assured white Georgians that any plan to "subsidize the child rather than the school" was lawful.[68]

In 1958, Ernest Vandiver became governor after promising white voters: "Neither my child nor your child will ever attend an integrated school during my administration. No, not one!"

Crowds packed into Henry Grady High School for the Sibley Commission's hearing on school desegregation, Atlanta, Georgia, March 23, 1960.

Afterwards, the legislature enacted tuition tax credits for families whose children attended private schools, barred using local property taxes to finance desegregated public schools, and empowered the governor to close either school districts or individual public schools as needed.[69] During this period, Atlanta's NAACP attorney Donald Hollowell, who advanced many of the court challenges to Georgia's school segregation, stated that he would not predict the outcome of any court case, but added that he fully expected the color line to fall.[70]

Facing a federal court order for the token desegregation of four Atlanta public schools, Governor Vandiver considered accepting virtual segregation, earning the outrage of political kingmaker Roy Harris, who declared: "If one little Negro is entitled to go to Henry Grady High School in Atlanta, then all Negroes are entitled to go to some high school with whites."[71] Vandiver tried having it both ways: he recommended bills to continue absolute segregation while creating a Committee on the Schools, later called the Sibley Commission, to explore best options.

Atlanta businessman and corporate attorney John Sibley led the new commission in holding public hearings across the state. Afterwards the Commission recommended that public schools remain open and, in effect, that the state manage a slow process of token desegregation: "Those who insist upon total segregation must face the fact that it cannot be maintained in public schools by state law." The report's plan was designed "to effectuate voluntary association." Recommended strategies included freedom of parental choice, local decisions for pupil placements and pupil transfers, and tuition grants to private schools—the pillars of Alabama's earlier Boutwell plan.[72]

In January 1961, shortly after two thousand angry whites surrounded the dormitory of Charlayne Hunter, one of two

THEREFORE THE MAJORITY RECOMMENDED THAT:
   The following constitutional amendments be proposed:
1. No child shall be forced to attend a school with a child of the opposite race; and that the child whose parents object to an integrated school be entitled to reassignment, tuition grants, or scholarship aid.
2. To provide for a uniform system of local units for the administration of the schools, and to allow any such unit to close schools within the unit or to reopen the school in accordance with the wishes of the majority of the qualified voters.
Legislation be enacted to provide:
3. For tuition grants or scholarships for students who wish to withdraw from an integrated school or whose school has been closed
4. That the existing teacher retirement system cover private as well as public school teachers.

5. That the General Assembly consider whether to close the public schools of Georgia to maintain total segregation or to follow a course designed to keep them open with as much freedom of choice as possible, through pupil placement, empowering each community to vote as to whether to close or continue public schools, and parent option (Parents could ask for reassignment or withdrawal with financial aid for education elsewhere)

Cover of the Sibley report, April 28, 1960.

Grady High School admits its first African American students, Lawrence Jefferson and Mary McMullen, Atlanta, Georgia, September 6, 1961. Photograph by Bill Wilson.

black students admitted to the University of Georgia in Athens,[73] Governor Vandiver announced he would follow the Sibley report. He proposed to repeal race-specific laws of massive resistance and promised every Georgia child "his God-given right to freedom of association" through a new amendment securing "the constitutional rights of school children to attend private schools of their choice in lieu of public schools" through public financing.[74]

In August 1961, two black students desegregated Atlanta's Henry Grady High School without incident. Atlanta's peaceful acceptance of token integration at Grady and the city's other all-white high schools became, in the words of the *New York Times*, a "new and shining example of what can be accomplished" in the

South. President John Kennedy said afterwards: "I strongly urge all communities which face this difficult transition to look closely at what Atlanta has done."[75] That one day in 1961 burnished the city's growing international reputation as the "City Too Busy to Hate," while in fact it set in motion a process of pupil assignments that preserved virtual segregation across the entire school system.[76]

In 1962, Georgia financed vouchers for more than fifteen hundred students in private schools. In addition, the legislature aided white teachers in leaving public for private schools by allowing them to remain in the state retirement system. None of the new laws specifically mentioned "race" or racial segregation. In the aftermath of its "shining example," the Atlanta school board routinely denied requests by scores of black parents to transfer their children to all-white schools. Attorney Donald Hollowell assured the public "we will appeal," but courtroom challenges could not catch up with the school board's delaying tactics. By December 1963, Dr. Martin Luther King Jr. publicly condemned "something strange and appalling"—not a single black child was attending Atlanta's all-white elementary schools and only 153 of more than 14,000 black high school students attended classes with whites.[77]

With each passing year throughout the 1960s, legal strategies and tools of resistance to *Brown* became less important in Atlanta

WSB-TV newsfilm clip of Abe Gallman reporting on developments in the ongoing legal battle over school desegregation, Atlanta, Georgia, January 30, 1970.

and other metropolitan areas as white flight to suburban counties increased—illuminating another highly effective option for preserving the "freedom of white people to choose not to go to school with negroes." Georgia's voucher program petered out after a couple of years—once it became obvious that the program would not survive review by the courts and after the discovery that many of the program's beneficiaries were already attending private schools.[78]

THE CITIZENS' COUNCIL

Dedicated to the maintenance of peace, good order and domestic tranquility in our Community and in our State and to the preservation of our States' Rights.

Vol. 1, No. 8   OFFICIAL PAPER OF THE CITIZENS' COUNCILS — MAY, 1956   Jackson, Mississippi

Strength Through Unity

We Can Be "Moderated" Right Into Total Chaos

Citizens' Councils Formed Into National Organization At Historic April Meeting

Sixty-five delegates from eleven southern states met in New Orleans at the Roosevelt Hotel on April 7th for the purpose of uniting the various responsible Citizen's Councils and other similar organizations into an interstate group.

Our Movement Expands
(an Editorial)

Praise Jackson Stand In Bus Segregation Verdict

Famous General Favors Segregation Of Troops

Mark Clark Puts Security Above Petty Politics

Southern Labor Taking Sides With The South

Recent Efforts To Force Federal Dictatorship

New Hampshire Getting Taste Of Race Problem

Influx Of Negro Soldiers Irks Yankee Community

A Grim Challenge

Front of The Citizens' Council, *Jackson, Mississippi, May 1956.*

The Limits of Lawsuits:
Toppling Voucher Programs
But Not Segregated Schools

By 1965, most voucher programs, which had been enacted only in Southern states, had been declared unconstitutional or were under serious attack, no matter whether the programs involved indirect expenditures such as tax credits or were shrouded in nonracial language. Each law financing private schools was soon invalidated by a federal court (or abandoned in the case of Georgia before it could be struck down) because the efforts were perceived to evade or disrupt public school desegregation and to "significantly encourage and involve the State in private discriminations."[79]

A vital component in states' strategies to preserve segregation, vouchers operated differently depending on state politics, federal court decisions, and the values and judgments of the strategy committees. Exchanging ideas and information, these committees functioned separately, shaped and reshaped by the dynamics of a state's political and business leadership and without a coordinated sectional effort.

In their final reports, most strategy committees adopted methods and means that evaded any exact definition of what preserving school segregation meant as an expression of racial subordination. Like Georgia Governor "No, Not One" Vandiver, states adapted to the reality that absolute or total segregation could not be preserved in the face of federal enforcement of *Brown*. Sooner or later, white leaders such as Tom P. Brady, the Mississippi politician credited with the idea of forming the Citizens' Council, were willing to accept virtual segregation. Others, including Alabama corporate attorney Forney Johnston, knew at the time of *Brown* that virtual segregation with its token exceptions could preserve white supremacy so long as conservative white leaders kept control of schools, politics, and the economy.[80]

Starting in the mid-1960s, civil rights lawyers were able to use new national anti-discrimination laws to challenge a wider range of white supremacist laws and practices. The civil rights movement moved away from the courtroom as the primary venue for creating change. Before *Brown,* the NAACP and other civil rights lawyers led the way by using the words of the Constitution to take down the wall of segregation, beginning in the schoolhouses, one student at a time. Privately, NAACP chief attorney Thurgood Marshall laid out the legal approach: "Those white crackers are going to get tired of having Negro lawyers beating 'em every day in court."[81] Publicly, it was the hallmark of attorneys such as Donald Hollowell, known in Georgia as "Mr. Civil Rights," to remain reserved and dignified—what Hollowell later remembered with a wink as "courtly"—using only federal filings to argue with white society about segregation, even as white state officials brazenly belittled, condemned, and harassed them.[82] This strategy confronted white stereotypes and rendered *Brown* as the law of the land, but alone it proved too slow and inadequate to halt relentless white efforts to stop change or to keep pace with growing black demands.

The emergence of the student movement and direct action as strategies for challenging private and public segregation was in part a reaction to the slow, back-and-forth pace of litigation. In some places, even "the twin avenues of civil rights protest—legal and direct action—did not have a catalytic effect" in advancing desegregation.

Horace T. Ward (center), shaking hands with A. T. Walden,
Donald Hollowell, Atlanta, Georgia, 1970.

By the middle of the 1960s, school desegregation was no longer
the civil rights spearhead. As Dr. Martin Luther King Jr. observed
about his own town: "In the absence of legal, political, economic,
and moral pressure, not even a city as enlightened as Atlanta is
likely to grant the Negro his constitutional rights."[83]

Most of the South's white leaders were discovering that a more
fluid definition of segregation was their most effective defense.

Opening Exercises at Maury High
Desegregation day in Norfolk, Va., 1959.

A black student sits alone in an "integrated" Virginia school auditorium in 1959.

Increasingly, they realized the efficacy of moving away from "No, not one" or a stand in the schoolhouse door toward strategies that could do almost as much as absolute segregation. As early as 1956, the founder of the Citizens' Council had suggested that members should redefine their way of life as far more than complete separation of the races: "Segregation represents the freedom to choose one's associates, Americanism, state sovereignty, and the survival of the white race."[84]

As for the public schools, it did not matter that all the tools for preserving segregation could not withstand the scrutiny of the federal courts or that the civil rights leaders were employing new strategies. A decade after *Brown*, the architects and advocates of private school vouchers had discovered the means to permit only a symbolic semblance of desegregation. If only by trial and error in some states, "Southern anti-integration efforts during the post-*Brown* era were more often characterized by creativity and flexibility than by obstinacy and intransigence."[85]

By the end of the 1965 school year, Alabama, Georgia, Louisiana, Mississippi, North Carolina, South Carolina, and Virginia—the seven states that had adopted voucher programs—maintained the South's lowest rates of school desegregation. That year, fewer than 2 percent of all black students in each of the seven states were attending public schools with white students.[86]

Milton Friedman and 'Government Schools'

In 1955, almost a year after Albert Boutwell released the Alabama legislative report proposing private school vouchers as a key element in his committee's plan of "freedom of choice," libertarian economist Milton Friedman of the University of Chicago published "The Role of Government in Education."[87] It introduced academicians to an economic rationale for school vouchers. Friedman believed parents would get the best education for their children when private schools competed for enrollment. Advancing a theory he and others would repeat over decades, Friedman argued that "competitive private enterprise is likely to be far more efficient in meeting consumer demands than nationalized enterprises" in education.[88]

Friedman's advocacy for a system of government-financed vouchers to replace "government schools," as he called them, was grounded in his free market beliefs. However, in a page-long footnote he acknowledged that essentially the same proposal "has recently been suggested in several states as a means of evading the Supreme Court ruling against segregation"—a development Friedman said came to his attention after he had largely completed his essay. The economist assured readers that he deplored segregation and racial prejudice, but he also opposed forced "non-segregation" no less than forced segregation. (Friedman also opposed a federal fair employment commission that would prohibit racial discrimination in private employment and, later, the 1964 Civil Rights Act's prohibition against racial discrimination by private businesses.[89])

Friedman acknowledged that vouchers would allow a system where there could be "exclusively white schools, exclusively colored schools, and mixed schools. Parents can choose which to send their children to." He was at best agnostic about ending segregation in schools. He noted that the government could decide to make public funds available to private schools only if they were segregated schools, as some Southern states proposed in 1955, or only if they were nonsegregated schools. His proposal for vouchers was "not therefore inconsistent with either forced segregation or forced nonsegregation."[90]

Had he cared enough to inquire about Southern segregation, Friedman would have discovered that many white supremacists had already adopted the same outlook and conceptual framework to make vouchers instrumental in maintaining segregated schools. A year earlier, in response to *Brown*, Mississippi politician Tom P. Brady gave a speech (later expanded into a book) that became an informal manifesto for the Citizens' Council and other Southern segregationists. In *Black Monday*, Brady wrote:

> The public school is a socialized or politically monopolized institution, and suffers from weakness inherent in all monopolies. The only thing that prevents the public school from decaying completely

Milton Friedman, 1977.

is the fact that it is not a complete monopoly. Local control of the school gives the taxpayer and parent some say in its management. . . . Nothing will do more to better education in America than the breaking of the public school trust. . . .

This is not a proposal to abolish public schools. It is a proposal to put them into competition with free enterprise schools, so they can prove their worth. And this can be done by the remission to parents of the taxes they are compelled to pay to support politically-controlled schools, in an amount comparable to what they pay for

African American students arriving without incident at Van Buren High School, Little Rock, Arkansas, September 1958. Photograph by John T. Bledsoe.

private schooling. The method of effecting this remission—whether by deduction from income taxes or allowances from local levies—is a technical matter; if the principle established that a parent has the right to buy the educational service he deems best for his child, the fiscal problem of tax remission could be solved.[91]

Similarly, the Alabama "freedom of choice" plan—the first segregation strategy report, published a year before Friedman's essay—was built on the foundational philosophy that when "members of a race are thereby deprived of access to a school attended by the other race, the result is attributable not to compulsion by the state but to the inconsistent choices of free citizens." As Alabama's Forney Johnston explained, under his segregation plan "the state is obliged to give effect to the desire of parents without compulsion against either side" or, as Milton Friedman wrote, without "either forced segregation or forced nonsegregation."

Johnston foresaw that his Alabama plan would lead to the same place Friedman envisioned—moving from a dual school system to a three-school system with "exclusively white schools, exclusively colored schools, and mixed schools." And Johnston was confident that, so long as white parents had access to vouchers for private schools and segregationist leaders established and implemented pupil placement, his plan would preserve segregation in some form for most white students in his state.[92]

Friedman's analysis not only echoed segregationist plans but helped to revive a new nonracial defense of segregation. Within four years of the publication of Friedman's essay, a large number of Southern segregationists were advancing the theory of individual freedom as the leading rationale for vouchers and school choice. Perhaps the most prolific, active disciple of this libertarian approach was Virginia newspaperman Leon Dure, who converted Friedman's advocacies into a constitutional argument for freedom of association.

As tactics of massive resistance began to fail in Virginia, Dure urged state leaders in 1958 to adopt school vouchers and his principles of freedom of choice or freedom of association as the most effective means for limiting desegregation. The plan offered every child "of whatever color, of whatever means" a voucher (called a "scholarship"). Echoing Johnston and Friedman, Dure argued that "the South accepts the right of all people to associate, but it insists on the right of all people not to associate." On these terms, Dure wrote, "the Southern white case is not compulsory segregation; it also is individual liberty," which he believed was protected in federal and state constitutions' guarantees of the right to assemble. Oliver Hill, the Virginia NAACP's leading attorney who had brought one of the original cases involved in *Brown*, told Dure that his proposal would do little more than mask racial discrimination.[93]

When Virginia's Perrow Commission issued its report, reversing the openly defiant tone and recommendations of earlier governors and legislatures, it embraced tactics of local control and freedom of association. As one politician wrote to Dure, there was now complete "agreement that the Freedom of Choice plan is . . . not based on segregation or integration but that any child in Virginia may obtain a tuition grant"—an equal opportunity to all children to freely disassociate.[94]

Dure also helped to convince white leaders in Georgia to reverse their approach for preserving segregated schools. Dure's frequent correspondence with John Sibley and others helped Governor Vandiver's administration understand how embracing "freedom of association" held the best promise for justifying and preserving virtually segregated schools. The exact language of the new state constitutional amendment approved by the white voters of Georgia stated: "Freedom from compulsory association at all levels of public education shall be preserved inviolate." During the same period, Louisiana's white leaders also attempted to rescue their strategies to resist desegregation through a similar approach.[95]

Just as Friedman adopted the term "mixed schools," the segregationists' favorite scare phrase for desegregated schools, diehard segregationists adopted Friedman's language. In 1964, the Mississippi administrator of the Citizens' Council, William Simmons, abandoned his earlier primary defense of segregated schools as a matter of constitutional "state rights" and began condemning the monopoly of "government schools." In the Council's newsletter, echoing both Brady and Friedman, Simmons wrote that public schools "can no longer be considered public—they have become government school systems." Afterwards, the White Citizens' Council focused primarily in Mississippi on developing a private school system of choice, as their leaders condemned government schools as "socialism in its purest form."[96]

Friedman never joined forces with segregationists, but he remained indifferent about how his libertarian economic arguments aided their strategies. Over several decades he continued to promote the concepts and framework that segregationists in the late 1950s and early 1960s believed were their best chance and best arguments. Long after Southerners abandoned their segregationist rhetoric, Friedman's advocacy shaped how future scholars, advocates, and the general public would see vouchers and "freedom of choice" as acts of consumerism rather than segregationist tactics. "For whites moving into the new suburbs," writes historian James Hardman Jr., the term "carried the popular consumer phrase 'choice,' and gave the impression that simple economic choice, not morally questionable racial prejudice, was behind the segregation in their communities."[97] It was a redefinition of choice that most of the South's private schools, even those started as "segregation academies," came to embrace and propagate as they persisted and expanded in the decades that followed.

can
we
afford
to
close
our
public
schools?

Inset above, the cover, and right, a page from December 1959 booklet, "Can We Afford to Close Our Public Schools?"

damage to taxpayers

THE taxpayers of the South have invested billions of dollars in school plants. Are these expensive plants to be left empty and idle and allowed to suffer the ravages of vandalism and decay?

In 1958-59 nine schools in Virginia were closed for part of the year and four schools in Arkansas were closed for the year. The taxpayers continued to pay the 734 teachers who were under contract, but were unable to perform the function for which they were being paid.

Proposals connected with legislation for closing schools usually contain provisions for remitting school taxes to parents to be used in defraying the cost of private schools. But it is unlikely they will be allowed to use the fine buildings we have built at public expense.

In many cases the sums paid by the state will not meet the cost of private schools. Thus, the parents' outlay for education will be materially increased. No one seems to have really studied this aspect of the problem.

There will be other losses. Many public schools have excellent opportunities for adult education. Shops, art studios, kitchens, clothing rooms, music studios provided with trained instructors are open to the adult public in the evenings. Large numbers of taxpayers have thus availed themselves of the opportunity to acquire new vocations, add

Challenging Tax Benefits of Segregated Private Schools

Civil rights organizations recognized during the 1960s the danger that governmental support posed in helping to build segregated systems of private schools even after the courts had dismantled voucher programs. These groups pushed the Internal Revenue Service (IRS) to deny tax-exempt applications of "segregation academies." This federal tax status enabled whites to reduce their taxable income when contributing to racially exclusionary private schools. But, in 1967, the IRS announced that it would grant tax deductions for contributions to any Southern private school, even self-avowed segregation academies, because "the school is private and does not have such degree of involvement with the political subdivision as has been determined by the courts to constitute State action for constitutional purposes."[98]

The Lawyers Committee for Civil Rights Under Law sued the IRS in 1969 and obtained a court order requiring it to "affirmatively determine" that a private school in Mississippi is not "operated on a racially segregated basis as an alternative to white students seeking to avoid desegregated public schools." The three-judge federal court found that the "tax benefits under the Internal Revenue Code mean a substantial and significant support by the Government to the segregated private school pattern."[99] After its ruling was affirmed without opinion by the U.S. Supreme Court, the court issued a permanent injunction restricting the IRS from granting a tax exemption to any and all Mississippi private schools that applied for the tax benefit.[100]

Afterwards, the IRS revoked the tax exemptions of more than one hundred private schools and scrutinized applications for tax exemption from others; however, it took eight years before the agency proposed specific administrative regulations to implement the nondiscrimination policy adopted in 1970. During this time, the IRS faced a backlash from private schools and their supporters,

School District	1960 Population Total and % of Negro	Public School Enrollment (A.D.A.)	Name of Private School	Enrollment in Private School*	Budget of Public School* (Total Disbursement, 1962-63)	Budget of Private School* (Estimate for Current Year)	Tuition Grants
NORFOLK CITY	304,869 S. 26.4%	W. 32,337 N. 17,578	Douglas MacArthur Academy (Tidewater Educ. Foundation, Inc.) Accredited by state	200*	$16,241,289	$60-100,000*	Yes
JAMES CITY COUNTY (also serves Williamsburg City)	11,539 co. N. 35.5% 6,832 city S. 13.7%	County: W. 1,833 N. 1,307	Jamestown Academy	100*	$1,026,619	$35-40,000*	Yes
HOPEWELL CITY	17,895 S. 16.7%	W. 3,274 N. 849	Chester Educ. Foun.Inc. (Bermuda Academy)	50* (1-4 grades)	$1,376,107	$15-25,000*	Yes
AMELIA COUNTY	7,815 N. 51.3%	W. 310 (1964-65) N. 1,073	Amelia School Foundation (Amelia Academy)	270*	$519,462	$75-100,000*	Yes
BRUNSWICK COUNTY	17,779 N. 58.7%	W. 1,100* (1964-65) N. 2,923	Brunswick Academy Association	660*	$1,328,366	$225,000*	Yes
CHESTERFIELD COUNTY	71,197 N. 13.3%	W. 15,000* N. 1,997	Tomahawk Academy	130-150*	$10,962,464	$26-30,000*	Yes
KING AND QUEEN COUNTY	5,889 N. 53.3%	W. 230* N. 851	York Academy	300*	$463,733	$90-115,000*	Yes
POWHATAN COUNTY	6,747 N. 39.7%	W. 459* N. 586	Huguenot Academy	550	$400,380	$152-207,000	Rec'd '63-'64, '65 unknown
SUSSEX COUNTY	12,411 N. 66.3%	W. 968 N. 2,239	Tidewater Academy, Inc.	85 (high school)	$911,843	$40,000*	Yes
SURRY COUNTY	6,220 N. 64.7%	W. None N. 1,085	Surry County School Foundation	548*	$459,078	$150-170,000	No (Prohibited court order)
WARREN COUNTY (Front Royal)	14,655 N. 9.2%	W. 1,857 N. 283	John S. Mosby Academy (accredited by state)	1,150	$518,495	$345-440,000	Yes
PRINCE EDWARD COUNTY	14,121 N. 39.9%	W. 6 (1964-65) N. 1,700*	Prince Edward School Foundation (accredited by state)	1,125*	$439,000*	$400,000*	No (Prohibited court order)
ALBEMARLE COUNTY (Charlottesville City)	30,969 co. N. 14.5% 29,427 city N. 19%	W. 4,136 co. N. 1,274 W. 3,964 city N. 1,136	Charlottesville Education Foundation (accredited by state)	700*	$1,910,733 co. 2,011,852 city	$210-300,000* 2 bldgs. valued $500-700,000	Yes

* estimated or projected from available data. These figures, particularly on budget, tend to be conservative.

*** There are currently 13 known private school systems in Virginia with a total of about 5,678 white pupils enrolled. New private school development known to be underway in Nottoway and Appomattox Counties and is suspected in Charlotte, Lunenburg, Greensville, and the Isle of Wight. Information on private schools in Virginia is not easy to come by. Facts about each school are obscured and the State Department of Education either knows little or is reluctant to release any information. Private schools are not required to be accredited in Virginia. They refuse to supply any significant data. The four private schools which are designated as accredited were those which were accredited as of the 1962-63 school year. A few others may have been accredited since.

Prepared - January 1965
by Edward Peeples, Instructor in Sociology, Medical College of Virginia.

13 Known Private Schools in Virginia Established since 1958 to Circumvent Desegregation, 1965. Chart by Edward H. Peeples.

including Southern members of Congress, and, in this political environment, went back and forth with proposed administrative procedures and congressional hearings. When the Nixon administration issued final guidelines, the Lawyers Committee, the U.S. Civil Rights Commission, and others criticized the IRS's rules, procedures, and enforcement as inadequate.[101]

Despite the regulation's shortcomings, a significant number of religious private schools in the South objected to the new IRS rules on the grounds of religious freedom, claiming that the government could not oversee their operations under any circumstances, even if they engaged in practices of segregation and racial discrimination. In 1983, the U.S. Supreme Court disagreed and upheld the application of the IRS rules on religious schools in a case involving Bob Jones University in South Carolina. Chief Justice Warren Burger wrote that "the Government has a fundamental, overriding interest in eradicating racial discrimination in education—discrimination that prevailed, with official approval, for the first 165 years of this Nation's constitutional history. That governmental interest substantially outweighs whatever burden denial of tax benefits places on petitioners' exercise of their religious beliefs."[102]

After *Bob Jones University v. United States*, the IRS required tax-exempt private schools to demonstrate nondiscriminatory policies and operations. But the requirements proved minimal—involving little more than adoption of a policy statement by the school's founders or board, publication of the policy (in brochures and catalogues), and some way of demonstrating that the school had abandoned total, absolute segregation.[103]

Private schools in the South began to publish nondiscrimination statements and many began a slow process of admitting a token number of black or other students of color. It was a replay of the most effective tactics that segregationists had deployed in the public schools several years earlier. This change did little more than end all-white segregation in order to sustain virtual segregation. The practices satisfied the IRS requirement and allowed subsequent federal administrations to claim that private schools had shown "clear and specific factual evidence" of nondiscrimination.

The private school movement grew rapidly. After the 1969 Supreme Court ruling that "every school district is to terminate dual school systems at once" in Mississippi,[104] white parents responded. From 1965 to 1980, private school enrollment increased by more than 200,000 students across the South—with about two-thirds of that growth occurring in the states that had created voucher programs.[105]

There were no government surveys reporting race or ethnicity for private school enrollment at the start of the 1980s, but the Southern Regional Council, which monitored the movement after *Brown,* estimated that virtually segregated private schools in the eleven states of the former Confederacy enrolled between 675,000 and 750,000 white students. When computed with overall enrollment data for those states, these estimates suggest that somewhere between 65 and 75 percent of the private school's white students were virtually segregated by the early 1980s.[106]

Overall, the Southern states' white flight from public schools in the wake of desegregation from 1940 through 1980 helped to quadruple the number of students attending segregated private schools. As Jason Morgan Ward aptly observed, "[T]he end of the Jim Crow era rendered *segregation*, like *white supremacy* before it, a doomed battle cry. But it was not a dead proposition."[107]

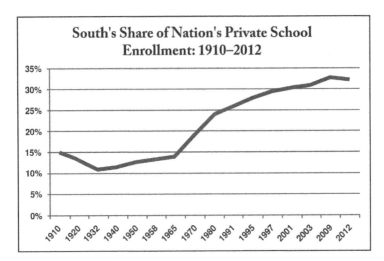

South's Share of Nation's Private School Enrollment, 1910–2012. Graph by the author based on computations of available U.S. Census data, 1910–2012.

The 'Post-Racialist' Standards Movement

Most of the South's private schools that started during massive resistance survived without vouchers—but with federal tax exemptions. Many increased their enrollments and resources as they embraced the old-line segregationists' nonracial language and reasoning. This transformation of stated purpose from preserving segregation to meeting children's needs for a quality education through choice involved an initial phase when headmasters and other promoters of private schools struggled to abandon their original meaning and adopt a new, nonracial script about motives and purposes.

Dr. T. E. Wannamaker, for example, founder of the South Carolina Independent School Association, explained in 1966 the reasons for his organization and schools: "We're here because we have convictions and we're going to stay. It's not token integration we're concerned about, but the effects mass integration will have on our schools in the future." Earlier, Wannamaker had described himself as "an old-time conservative. I believe it's heredity first and environment second. Many (Negroes) are little more than field hands." In 1970, he became the first leader of the Southern Independent School Association.[108] An Alabama private school advocate told a journalist in 1969, "We really didn't do it on account of segregation. We done it for a better education."[109]

By the 1970s, as many public schools in the South were being desegregated for the first time, promoters of private schools were developing a more consistent line of reasoning: the schools may have begun over the "racial question," but were now operating to provide "quality education." "I've been fighting to take the race question out of the Independent Schools," a member of the Louisiana Private School Association said in 1973. "I've run a segregated school for 33 years. . . . I want nice people in my school. We're trying to sell quality education."[110]

The headmaster of Prince Edward Academy (which five years earlier had been denied the continued benefit of vouchers and tax credits due to racial discrimination) told a researcher: "This school came into being because we love our children and want the best education in a controlled environment." A leader of Louisiana's private schools expanded this new language of transition: "I think people would be able to accept integration if it did not mean lowering of academic and moral standards. But they know it means it; therefore, they resort to private schools." And the head of the Alabama Independent School Association told researcher Rose Gladney in 1972: "Our primary interest is educating people basically of like

Prince Edward Academy, Farmville, Virginia, ca. 1962.
Photograph by Edward H. Peeples.

learning capacities. We adopt a school system to meet their needs.
. . . The real historical importance of the movement is not one of
segregation or integration. It's academically important."

It was left to a student in one of the private schools that Gladney
visited to be explicit about the white supremacist message he heard
from administrators, promoters, and perhaps family: "Niggers are
dumb; can't learn. And when you have a majority of low standard
in a school, they will pull all the rest down. It is not really a race
issue, just a matter of lowering standards."[111]

Many private schools operated by churches also began to justify
their existence through the imperative of religious education. "Religion is an integral part of the Independent School movement,"
said the director of the Louisiana Independent School Association. "We're developing a pseudo-parochial system where there's
a fixed religion we feel we want."[112] These often became Christian
schools that turned "in every particular around Bible teachings
and interpretations."[113]

Whatever the nonracial rationale—economic freedom, better
education, religious instruction—the vast majority of the South's
private schools were established when it became clear locally that
federal law would require some form of desegregation. By the start
of the 1980s, the character of most of these private schools was set.
"These are schools for whites," wrote the authors of *The Schools that
Fear Built* in 1976. "The common thread that runs through them all,
Christian, secular, or otherwise, is that they provide white ground
to which blacks are admitted only on the school's terms if at all."[114]

For God and Private Schools

Following the 1980 election of Ronald Reagan, private schools throughout the nation received federal support and endorsement as never before. The Reagan administration justified proposed federal assistance to private schools as a means for advancing high quality education along with diversity and pluralism. The administration waffled on whether to support Bob Jones University's claim that religion gave it the right to discriminate on the basis of race even while receiving tax exemption. "I was under the impression," Reagan said, "that the problem of segregated schools had been settled, that we have desegregation."[115]

In 1981, Reagan's secretary of education testified in support of tax credit vouchers for private schools as "an expansion of educational opportunities for all Americans." In 1983, Reagan became the first president to send Congress legislation for federal tax credits to finance private schools. The proposed "Educational Opportunity and Equity Act," the administration argued, would benefit a wide range of students, including low-income children of color, and more broadly would "promote diversity in education and the freedom of individuals to take advantage of it, and to nurture the pluralism in American society which this diversity fosters." School segregation was a thing of the past, said Reagan, and private schools were the engines of diversity.[116]

Reagan linked his tax credit bill with an imperative to return religion to schools. "I don't think God should ever have been expelled from the classroom," he declared at a news conference in which he defended his support of private schools, including

Dr. Jerry Falwell holds a religious rally, Tallahassee, Florida, 1980. Photograph by Mark T. Foley. An accompanying note reads, "Dr. Jerry Falwell, from Lynchburg, Virginia, acknowledges ministers in the audience here Monday as some 1,000 gathered on the steps of the capitol for an 'I Love America Rally.' Falwell will be taking the program to all 50 state capitals in an effort to revive the spirit of America under God and promote a moral rebirth at the seats of government in each state."

religious schools. The president's remarks echoed a long line of Southern segregationists who had justified the growth of private schools on religious grounds, especially after 1961 when the U.S. Supreme Court outlawed a New York statute that required public school students to recite an official Christian prayer.[117]

White churches started private academies in the wake of court-ordered desegregation, with religion and segregation often inter-mingling in the schools' stated purpose. In Prince Edward County, Virginia, many white clergy supported closing the public schools, their churches provided white-only space, and their curricula were built around church teachings. "Our people—supporters of the Independent schools—are convinced God is behind us," asserted the head of the Louisiana segregated private schools in the early 1970s. "If you don't include that aspect, you're missing a good part of the motivation behind this movement. People believe wholeheartedly that God doesn't want us to mix."[118]

Looking across the South in 1974, Rose Gladney, a young scholar whose family had been actively involved in setting up a segregation academy in Homer, Louisiana, saw how most adults involved in private schools had merged racial segregation, quality education, and religion into one rationale. "The teachings of the academies," Gladney sadly observed, "hope to ensure that there will be people who think there is a need because they will have been taught, for at least another generation, that love of God, love of their white skins, and love of quality education cannot be separated."[119]

President Reagan transformed a "love of white skin" into a color-blind doctrinal belief that individual freedom of choice in schooling created diversity and opportunity for all in an era without segregation. Reagan became the nation's primary voice for why and how government should support private schools, and, as a former actor and California governor, his own past and national leadership obscured the original role and rationales of Southern white supremacists from public memory.

In 1984, in renominating Reagan, the Republican Party's education platform included support for the right to pray in public schools, opposition to busing for desegregation, passage of tuition tax credits for private schools, and redirecting billions of federal funds dedicated to assist low-income students in public schools into vouchers for private schools. It was the first time a national

Claiborne Academy, Claiborne Parish, Louisiana, May 26, 2009. Photograph by Billy Hathorn.

political party endorsed school vouchers. In his State of the Union address fourteen months later, President Reagan declared: "We must continue the advance by supporting discipline in our schools, vouchers that give parents freedom of choice; and we must give back to our children their lost right to acknowledge God in their classrooms."[120] It was the first time a U.S. president expressly advocated for school vouchers before a joint session of Congress. Without attribution, the views and tools of Southern segregationists had become the official position of the national Republican Party and the Reagan presidency.

No to 'Racial-Mixing,' Yes to Vouchers

At the end of the Reagan administration, almost thirty-five years after *Brown*, enrollment in the South's private schools continued to grow in absence of any significant new government financial support.[121] Some schools created in defiance of desegregation struggled and failed, but most survived by embracing other stated purposes for their existence and by maintaining their tax-exempt status—a benefit that required most to enroll just enough children of color to avoid total segregation while preserving a culture of "schools for whites."[122]

Since the 1960s, white flight from urban public systems such as Atlanta's had maintained and extended segregated patterns in private tax-exempt schools and in suburban public schools. On both sides of the Mason-Dixon line, many white middle-class parents had escaped the mandates of school desegregation by moving into suburban neighborhoods where residential patterns of racial isolation and economics provided virtually segregated public schools. This suburban constituency helped to sustain Nixon and Reagan policies in blocking inter-district desegregation plans.[123]

Earlier segregationists had foreseen the importance of district lines. In 1955, Forney Johnston, one of the architects of the Alabama three-school "freedom of choice" plan, identified "ordinary and customary geographical districting" as a primary tool for defeating *Brown*. His strategies cast a very long shadow. Examining school data from 1988 to 1990, a national study concluded "that white families are fleeing public schools with large concentrations of poor minority schoolchildren. In addition, the clearest flight appears to be away from poor black schoolchildren."[124]

The patterns persisted. Based on data from 1998, scholars Sean Reardon and Jon Yun found that the "South ha[d] the greatest segregation between the public and private sector of any region—white and Asian private school enrollment rates are more than three times greater than black rates in the South, and more than double Latino rates."[125] They also concluded that "the strongest predictor of white private enrollment is the proportion of black students in the area."[126]

Drawing upon the 2000 Census, Duke University scholar Charles Clotfelter found that private schools were continuing to foster racial separation and isolation in K–12 education in the South,

Rally at state capitol protesting the admission of the "Little Rock Nine" to Central High School, Little Rock, Arkansas, August 20, 1959. Photograph by John T. Bledsoe.

especially in non-metropolitan areas: "Combined with the general stability or growth of private enrollments in the South since 1970, these findings suggest that private schools were playing much the same role in non-metropolitan counties of the South in 1999–2000 as they were shortly after desegregation."[127]

During this time, Milwaukee and Cleveland became limited, urban experiments in voucher programs in northern states, as some white liberals suggested that vouchers might offer a way to break up what they came to believe were intractable problems faced by low-income public schoolchildren. It was also the era when state governments began establishing programs to finance attendance in private schools, especially through tax credit vouchers. This new initiative reached into every part of the nation, but mostly the South, including all of the states where segregationists had established vouchers.[128]

The U.S. Supreme Court began to bless these developments. As early as 1973, Justice William Rehnquist became the first member of the Court to issue a dissent from a school desegregation case relying on the precedent of *Brown*. In a case concerning school segregation in Denver, he condemned the Court's opinion for requiring a school district to advance desegregation—employing the old scare word, "racial mixing"—where there were "neutrally drawn boundary lines" that sustained segregation.[129] Barely a year after the *Bob Jones* decision held that religious private schools could not hold a tax exemption and discriminate on the basis of race, the Supreme Court slammed shut the courthouse door on those seeking to challenge the IRS's weak enforcement. Parents of twenty-five black public school children sued the IRS, charging that its standards and procedures were inadequate to fulfill its obligation to deny tax-exempt status to racially discriminatory private schools. In 1984, the Court held that the parents had no standing to bring such a suit.[130]

With the appointment of other justices across more than three decades, the Court increasingly refused to require school districts to use any method of desegregation that proved effective in dismantling the dynamics of separation. By 2007, the Court had turned *Brown* on its head as a precedent for backing public school districts' voluntary efforts to desegregate. Chief Justice John Roberts wrote that *Brown* commanded school districts to avoid using race as a consideration, even for the purpose of recognizing and diminishing public school segregation. "When it comes to using race to assign children to schools," Roberts wrote without doubt or irony, "history will be heard."[131]

As the Court stymied effective strategies for desegregating public schools, Justice Anthony Kennedy led it in unleashing private schools from constitutional restraints for receiving taxpayer funds. Arizona's program of tax credit vouchers allowed individuals and corporations to give tax dollars to private schools instead of paying them to the state—a scheme similar to those the Court had outlawed in prior cases, including in Prince Edward County, Virginia, in the 1960s. Kennedy, in a majority opinion, held that tax credit vouchers did not involve public funds or any state action that the Bill of Rights would prohibit. "While the State, at the outset, affords the opportunity to create and contribute," Kennedy wrote, "the tax credit system is implemented by private action and with no state intervention."[132]

With few federal restraints, legislatures have expanded these programs or established new forms of vouchers, such as educational savings accounts that deposit state and local per-pupil expenditures into a personal account for a child's parents to use toward private

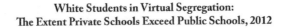

White Students in Virtual Segregation:
The Extent Private Schools Exceed Public Schools, 2012

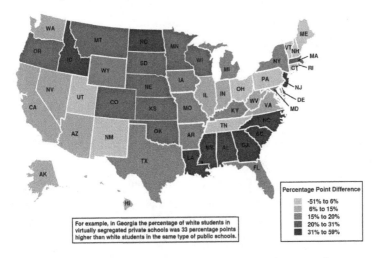

Map based on author's computations of National Center for Education Statistics data, 2012. Courtesy of the Southern Education Foundation.

schooling or to supplement home-schooling.

Patterns of virtual segregation have stayed remarkably high in private schools. As recently as 2012, 43 percent of the nation's private school students attended virtually all-white schools—schools where white students comprise 90 percent or more of the enrollment. That year, half of the fifty states had a majority of private school students attending virtually segregated schools.[133]

Despite white flight, virtual segregation for white students was far more substantial in private schools than in public schools, especially in the South. In 2012, 63 percent of white students in South Carolina's private schools were virtually segregated compared with only 5 percent of white students in South Carolina's public schools. Private schools were almost twelve times more likely to enroll white students in virtually segregated schools in 2012 than were the state's public schools.

In Mississippi, white students attending private schools were almost four times more likely to be in virtually segregated schools than public school students. More than seven out of ten white students in Mississippi's private schools attended schools where 90 percent or more of the enrollment was white. In the state's public schools, the rate was 15 percent. In Louisiana, 52 percent of the white students in private schools were virtually segregated in 2012, but only 14 percent for white public school students.

This new era of vouchers emerged as public schools across the nation experienced a substantial increase in the numbers of low-income students and students of color. Completing a trend that began in the 1980s, low-income students (those eligible for free or reduced lunch) became a majority of the South's public school-children in 2006; in 2009, the South's public schools also had a majority of students of color. By 2013, more than 50 percent of the nation's public schoolchildren were from low-income families and almost half were children of color.[134]

Changing patterns, most evident in the nation's cities, spread to the suburbs. In 2011, 40 percent of public schoolchildren in the nation's suburban districts were low-income; the rates were 45 percent or higher in suburbs in the West and the South. During the 2000s, the number of suburban poor exceeded the number in the nation's cities for the first time. Similarly, with a huge increase in Hispanic children, suburban school districts began educating a student population in which students of color comprised more than 40 percent. At the same time, African Americans moved into suburban counties surrounding central cities (such as Atlanta) in record numbers.[135]

This new diversity in suburban school-age populations did not result in major increases in integrated schools. Instead, old habits resurfaced that involved shifting residential segregation, white flight into exurbs, localities attempting to secede from majority-black public school districts, and the states' rebirth of vouchers for private schools. Legislatures failed to increase public school funding to meet the huge challenges of educating a majority of schoolchildren who are low-income and nonwhite, especially in the South and West where most voucher programs have emerged.[136]

New Token Students of Choice

Overall trends have obscured a small, inclusive change in the color line for admission to private schools amid a more pronounced, underlying pattern of racial exclusion. Frequently, white private schools have chosen Asian or Pacific Island children to break their completely segregated enrollment in order to reach a token level of diversity for an IRS tax exemption. These students have family ancestries from countries including China, Vietnam, Korea, Japan, India, the Philippines, and various islands of the Pacific. In 2012, Asian American students comprised 5.8 percent of the nation's private school enrollment—a number slightly above the percentage of the Asian school-age population. Only white students and students with Asian ancestries were in private schools in numbers that exceeded or generally matched their representation in the school-age population. In forty-two states, the percentage of Asian students in private schools exceeded the state's percentage of school-age Asian children.[137]

This development stands in sharp contrast to the history of discrimination that Asians have experienced, especially in California and the South, and makes Asian students stand out among students of color attending private schools. The explanation for this shift seems grounded in at least three factors: since the late 1980s, Asian households have had the nation's highest median income (more than $11,500 above non-Hispanic white household income in 2012); since at least the 1990s, Asian students have had the nation's highest scores on standardized tests; and more than three generations after World War II, some whites may find the lighter skin color of

Asian Americans more acceptable according to racist hierarchies.[138]

Asian children usually comprise a small minority of a private school's enrollment. Their presence often serves to increase a school's performance on college entrance exams—enabling schools to promote evidence of quality education while avoiding an all-white enrollment that could jeopardize their tax exemption. Asian Americans' admission, however, does not change the reality of most private schools as "schools for whites."[139]

Increased token admission of Asian children obscures the fact that the patterns of virtual segregation and exclusion in private

Under-Representation of Students of Color in Private Schools, 2012

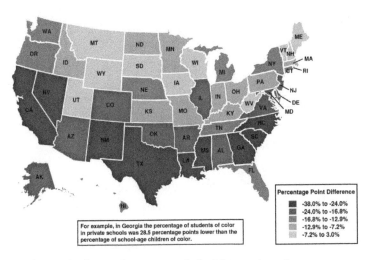

For example, in Georgia the percentage of students of color in private schools was 28.5 percentage points lower than the percentage of school-age children of color.

Percentage Point Difference
- -38.0% to -24.0%
- -24.0% to -16.8%
- -16.8% to -12.9%
- -12.9% to -7.2%
- -7.2% to 3.0%

Students of color in this map include African American, Hispanic, and Native American children. Map based on author's computations of National Center for Education Statistics Private School Survey, 2011–2012 and Census-based school-age population estimates.

Percentages of White School Children Attending "Exclusionary" Schools, 2012

List of the Ten States with Largest Difference in Rates between Private and Public Schools

State	Private School Percentage	Public School Percentage
South Carolina	84%	11%
Delaware	72%	4%
Mississippi	81%	17%
Oregon	78%	22%
North Carolina	73%	18%
Oklahoma	55%	4%
Louisiana	66%	18%
Georgia	63%	14%
Alabama	74%	27%
Nevada	47%	3%

Table based on author's computations of National Center for Education Statistics data, 2012.

schools are considerably larger for under-represented racial and ethnic groups: African Americans, Hispanics, and Native Americans. In 2012, two-thirds of white students in U.S. private schools attended virtually "exclusionary schools"—schools where African American, Hispanic, and Native American children were 10 percent or less of total enrollment. In thirty of the fifty states, 70 percent or more of all white students attending private schools were in such schools.[140]

This "exclusionary" pattern is not unique to private schools. Some public schools also have extremely low rates of enrollment of

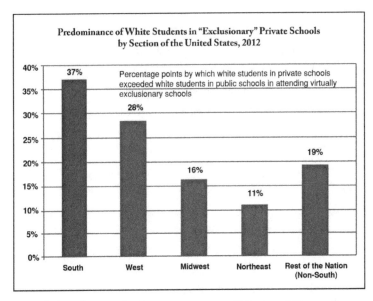

Graph based on author's computations of National Center for Education Statistics data, 2012.

African American, Hispanic, and Native American children. But, private schools in forty-seven of the fifty states have far higher rates of this kind of "exclusionary" enrollment than do public schools. In twenty-six of these states, the rates of "exclusionary" schooling in private schools were more than 25 percentage points higher than rates in public schools. The largest differences were in Southern states. For example, 84 percent of white students in South Carolina private schools attended schools where African American, Hispanic, and Native American students together comprised only 10 percent or less of the private school enrollment. But only 11 percent of the white students attending public schools in South Carolina were in similarly "exclusionary" schools.

Each Southern state that adopted voucher schemes in the era of massive resistance to *Brown*, except for Virginia, appears on the top ten list for exclusionary schooling, and Virginia was not far away. Like Virginia, Arkansas (where vouchers were tried temporarily in Little Rock) also had a gap of 34 percentage points. All Southern states, except West Virginia, had a gap of 20 percentage points or larger. In West Virginia, the gap was 10 percentage points.

With the re-emergence of vouchers, the overwhelming majority of white students attending the nation's private schools continue to attend "schools for whites." The geographies where segregationists invented and implemented vouchers to resist *Brown* remain the places with greatest patterns of "exclusionary" private schools—assuring their white students that they do not attend school with any more than a token number of under-represented students of color. In 2012, the percentage of white students attending "exclusionary" private schools in the South exceeded the percentage in similar public schools in the South by 37 percentage points. This gap was double that of the rest of the nation.

Lingering Facets of Jim Crow Segregation

States that adopted the first voucher plans in the 1950s and 1960s were forced by federal courts to abandon the laws and practices of complete separation of the races in schools and other public places. Yet Jim Crow laws were far from the only manifestations of segregation. The "better citizens" (as upper-class white supremacists were often called) were willing to accept token desegregation because of their belief that white supremacy and racial superiority did not place each and every white person always above "a negro of intelligence and good character."[141]

The practice of permitting virtual segregation or token desegregation was widespread before and during Jim Crow. Often, the all-white Democratic primary was not all-white. "In county after county," V. O. Key Jr. wrote in *Southern Politics in State and Nation*, "a few Negroes have voted for many years in Democratic primaries conducted under white-primary rules." The practice of holding virtually segregated primaries was particularly common where African Americans comprised a small proportion of the population.[142]

Similarly, Southern justice was segregated, and "after 1900, essentially no blacks sat on Southern juries." But, as civil rights and civil liberties attorney Charles ("Chuck") Morgan noted in the 1960s, "[T]he names of a token number of Negroes are often included on jury rolls." These token blacks—hand-picked by white jury commissioners from the few African Americans deemed acceptable—seldom served since they could be struck by prosecutors or defense lawyers.[143]

In their analysis of the South's segregationist leaders during massive resistance, historians Matthew Lassiter and James Hershman characterize segregationists as either caste-based or class-based. The caste-based defended complete segregation or exclusion on the belief that "all black people were inherently inferior to all white people." Understanding that absolute segregation was unnecessary to maintain a rule of white supremacy, the class-based segregationist (sometimes described as "moderate segregationists") conceded that "perhaps a few black people could be accepted into white institutions."[144]

The ambitions of politicians such as George Wallace and Ernest Vandiver muddled the division between caste and class, but the contrasting definitions illustrate that segregation was not defined as only a total, absolute exclusion of all African Americans or other people of color from the spaces—including schools—occupied by whites. Southern laws were often written that way, but reality was different. Affluent leaders of the most successful strategies for defeating desegregation demonstrated a class-based acceptance of virtual segregation and worked to preserve it. They anticipated the long-term possibility of ending absolute segregation and empowering leaders of local schools to justify virtual segregation through nonracial language, traditional school attendance boundaries, and neutral-sounding educational admissions standards, although it is doubtful that many realized how powerful class-based terms would resonate in suburban desegregation politics decades later.[145]

The layered dimensions of segregation and exclusion are also illuminated by school segregation laws outside the South—in states that practiced *de jure* segregation well into the twentieth century—including the law invalidated by the *Brown* decision in Topeka, Kansas.[146]

Linda Brown Smith, Ethel Louise Belton Brown, Harry Briggs Jr., and Spottswood Bolling Jr. during press conference at Hotel Americana, June 9, 1964. Photograph by Al Ravenna.

All the attention drawn to the South's massive resistance eclipsed notice of how the Kansas school segregation law differed by excluding black children from all white schools *only* in cities with a population over 15,000. The Kansas statute allowed boards of education in larger municipalities to decide if they should establish absolute segregation in those places where the number of African American children might exceed virtual or token segregation in a public school. In all other areas of Kansas with small black populations, demographic patterns assured an acceptable level of virtual segregation.

Kansas population data illustrates how the law preserved virtual segregation in most of the state and absolute segregation where there was more than a token number of black children. From 1890 through 1950, Kansas's black population never reached 4 percent of the state's total, with the vast majority of black Kansans living in and around a few cities. In 1950, there were 73,158 African Americans among more than 1.9 million Kansans. Almost three-fourths of the state's black population resided in five counties where the state's largest cities were empowered to enact total segregation. All but one did. Elsewhere in Kansas in 1950, twenty thousand African Americans were spread among 1.3 million whites across one hundred counties, ensuring the maintenance of virtual segregation without the force of law.[147]

In 1951, when Linda Brown's father sued to desegregate her school system, Topeka (pop. 80,000) required absolute segregation in neighborhood elementary schools, undoing the virtual segregation that demographic trends assured to most white parents elsewhere in Kansas. In other words, Kansas's law had the same intent as Southern laws—to maintain some form of segregation in all cases—although it did not establish absolute segregation as the default. That was implemented only when virtual segregation could not be maintained in practice.

Arizona also had a school segregation law—in some public high schools—triggered whenever twenty-five or more "pupils of African race" registered. In these situations, 15 percent of the voters in the school district could initiate a referendum to require the local school board to "segregate the pupils of the African race from pupils of the Caucasian race." In other words, the presence of twenty-five black students in a high school could set in motion a process for absolute segregation.

In adjoining New Mexico, the law permitted the separation of "pupils of African descent" into separate classrooms in the same buildings if the school boards decided "it was for the best advantage of the school." The state allowed a local school board to decide what number of students might endanger virtual segregation, although it did permit the local jurisdiction to avoid the cost of building a separate school to implement absolute segregation.

Wyoming law gave school boards and superintendents power to enforce absolute segregation whenever there were fifteen or more "colored children" within a district. Since the large majority of Wyoming's schools were small, the numerical calculation of what number might threaten virtual segregation was also quite small. Until 1949, local jurisdictions in Indiana could decide to institute absolute segregation under a law used almost exclusively in larger cities where the percentage of black population jeopardized virtual segregation.[148]

These laws were different from those in the South because they assumed a different starting point. Before *Brown*, non-Southern states started with virtual segregation and went to the absolute form when necessary, while Southern states started with absolute segregation and went to virtual segregation when required by *Brown*. Wherever, school segregation was a multifarious exclusion without an exact shape or defining measure. As practiced, segregation always revolved around what a white-controlled legislature, white constituency, or white-controlled institution considered minimally acceptable. Contemporary private school patterns and practices—that state and federal governments have come to tolerate and often support with public funds—appear for what they are: legacies of class-based Southern segregation used to evade *Brown* and multi-dimensional segregation of non-Southern states before *Brown*.

Desegregation's Future

During the heyday of the first era of school vouchers, Dr. Martin Luther King Jr. decried that "token integration is little more than token democracy, which ends up with many new evasive schemes and it ends up with new discrimination, covered up with such niceties of complexity."[149] King's words have proven prophetic, although he could not have foreseen how dramatically the icons and language of the movement he led would be used, even by his own lineage, to develop and advance the tools and strategies that segregationists of his day thought could defeat the promise of *Brown*.

Today's advocates of school vouchers are not the first to attempt to graft the words and imagery of King and the civil rights movement onto their reactionary cause. As early as 1988, Rev. Jerry Falwell of the Moral Majority declared to a gathering of all-white, conservative male ministers in Atlanta that "Martin Luther King is everybody's American hero."[150] But the school choice and voucher movement is remarkable in replicating so closely the primary strategies and tactics of Southern segregationists while claiming the righteous mantle of the people and movement who fought against those segregationists.

One reason school choice proponents have appropriated civil rights rhetoric may relate to the fact that there is little evidence that vouchers improve the education of low-income children or children of color.[151] Voucher advocates' strongest arguments invoke social justice as well as freedom in order to legitimate school choice as more than a consumerist mindset and to obscure the factual results.[152]

A larger part of the explanation surely lies in forgetting what little was known and understood about segregationists such as

Alabama's Forney Johnston and Albert Boutwell, Georgia's John Sibley, North Carolina's Thomas Pearsall, and Virginia's Garland Gray. In current memory, George Wallace remains the image of the diehard segregationist—standing defiantly to assure not one black child in any white school. The images, language, and cruel tactics of Wallace and Birmingham's "Bull" Connor remain vivid in the lingering American mind, but not the strategic, behind-the-scenes work of South Carolina's Marion Gressette.

Yet, the Southern states' first plan for defeating court-ordered desegregation, the one that Johnston and Boutwell devised in 1954 in Alabama, is exactly what today's advocates and supporters of vouchers seek to implement: no compulsory "race-mixing" in schools and no mention of any intent to discriminate. What could be more American than the freedom of parents to choose their children's school—private or public—with public financial support?

The Boutwell plan also aimed to remove from the state constitution and statutes any right of education for a child and any obligation to fund education. Instead, a state was to "foster education of its citizens in a manner and extent consistent with its available resources, *and* the willingness and ability of the individual student [emphasis added]."[153] The plan authorized white school officials to decide "the eligibility, admission, and allocation of pupils, including the power to refuse admission to individuals or groups whose deficiencies in scholastic aptitude would compel undue lowering of school standards."[154] The state was to provide vouchers and tax funds to private schools to increase school choice options.

The primary components of segregationist plans developed in the 1950s and 1960s by Southern states are today the main objectives of policymakers and advocates leading the movement for school choice and vouchers.[155] No less remarkable, the segregation

Children and adults picketing for school integration, West Point, Mississippi, ca. 1965.

that Forney Johnston envisioned in his tripartite school system was also foreseen by economist Milton Friedman, who considered it an acceptable consequence of his goal of managing the country's education systems through market forces.

The nation's lack of memory has done far more than encourage the acceptance as racially neutral the economic and social arguments of voucher advocates, who blithely use the language of civil rights to advance the tools of segregationists. The nation has lost an understanding of class-based segregation as a general but not absolute condition for preserving racial superiority. This country also has failed to remember that school segregation laws outside the South embodied the same bifurcated notion of absolute and virtual segregation, although applied to different locales and demographies. More disturbing is the current wide acceptance of segregation as a part of an American way of schooling that merits public funding.

Public school teachers and supporters picket in Milwaukee, Wisconsin, April 24, 2018. Photo by Charles Edward Miller.

At the same time, the legal meaning and force of racial discrimination in civil rights enforcement and tax policy has shrunk to such an extent that courts, the public, and policy makers often recognize discrimination in private schools only if a person or institution sounds like an old-style segregationist who says "No, not one." Even some of the nation's most prominent public scholars have failed to grasp how, despite past court rulings, the strategies of virtual segregation continue today as prevailing practice among religious and nonreligious private schools with tax exemptions.[156]

The U.S. Supreme Court has declared as law of the land that private schools cannot enjoy the benefits of exemptions from federal income tax, much less receive tax credits and direct government funding, while engaging in racial discrimination, even when motivated by claims of religious freedom. But, the federal government's current standards and practices of enforcement accept as valid and true on its face any private school's public pledge of nondiscrimination in admission practices and operations, so long as the school has no formal or written policies to the contrary and does not maintain absolute, complete "No, not one" segregation. And parents of public school children cannot go to federal court to challenge the lack of robust, effective enforcement.

This faux policy of anti-discrimination has permitted a majority of private schools across the nation to maintain what strategic Southern segregationists sought to achieve after *Brown*—virtual segregation and exclusion of children of color. Recall that two-thirds of white students attending the nation's private P–12 schools are in institutions where African American, Hispanic, and Native American children constitute 10 percent or less of the student body. These white schools are exercising "school choice" to decide which and how many children of color to admit—in token numbers and on terms, values, and motives inherited from strategic segregationists who, as Julian Bond noted, "dared not say out loud" their true goals.[157]

More than half of the nation's states have adopted some form of vouchers to support private schools, portending that virtual segregation and exclusion will be sustained over time. And the federal government is moving closer than ever to establishing a program of direct or tax credit vouchers to support private schools on whatever terms are acceptable to the states. Nor is there serious consideration of revising the standards and practices that have already permitted many states to erect the scaffolding of a private–public school system first put forward by Alabama segregationists in 1954.

By failing to grasp the history of the struggles and tactics against Southern school desegregation, the nation has come to recognize segregation and racial superiority only in those private schools that are absolutely all-white. The looming danger lies in legitimizing and

School Choice Programs in the United States, 2019

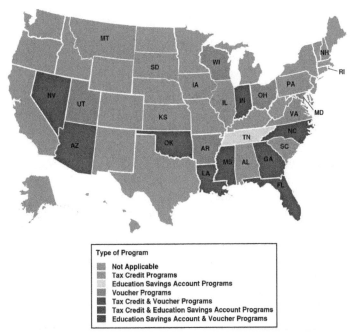

Type of Program

- Not Applicable
- Tax Credit Programs
- Education Savings Account Programs
- Voucher Programs
- Tax Credit & Voucher Programs
- Tax Credit & Education Savings Account Programs
- Education Savings Account & Voucher Programs

Map by the author. Courtesy of the Southern Education Foundation.

advancing a system of segregation and exclusion in education that is not called by its name. Even if most Americans find repugnant the absolute separation of the races that George Wallace defiantly championed as destiny in 1963, his words have transformed into a prophesy about schools across the nation that rings true by the most accurate, historical definition of the term: "segregation now . . . segregation tomorrow . . . segregation forever." ❧

Recommended Resources

Text

Batchelor, John E. *Race and Education in North Carolina: From Segregation to Desegregation.* Baton Rouge: Louisiana State University Press, 2015.

Bolton, Charles C. *The Hardest Deal of All: The Battle Over School Integration in Mississippi, 1870–1980.* Jackson: University Press of Mississippi, 2005.

Brown-Nagin, Tomiko. *Courage to Dissent: Atlanta and the Long History of the Civil Rights Movement.* New York: Oxford University Press, 2011.

Carl, Jim. *Freedom of Choice: Vouchers in American Education.* Santa Barbara, CA: Praeger, 2011.

Carpenter II, Dick M., and Krista Kafer. *"A History of Private School Choice."* Peabody Journal of Education 87, no. 3 (2012): 336–350.

Crespino, Joseph. *In Search of Another Country: Mississippi and the Conservative Counterrevolution.* Princeton, NJ: Princeton University Press, 2009.

Driver, Justin. *The Schoolhouse Gate: Public Education, the Supreme Court, and the Battle for the American Mind.* New York: Pantheon Books, 2018.

Gladney, Margaret Rose. *"I'll Take My Stand: The Southern Segregation Academy Movement."* PhD diss., University of New Mexico, 1974.

Klarman, Michael J. *Brown v. Board of Education and the Civil Rights Movement.* New York: Oxford University Press, 2007.

Lassiter, Matthew D. *The Silent Majority: Suburban Politics in the Sunbelt South.* Princeton, NJ: Princeton University Press, 2006.

Lassiter, Matthew D., and Andrew B. Lewis, eds. *The Moderates' Dilemma: Massive Resistance to School Desegregation in Virginia.* Charlottesville: University of Virginia Press, 1998.

O'Brien, Thomas V. *The Politics of Race and Schooling: Public Education in Georgia, 1900–1961.* Lanham, MD: Lexington Books, 1999.

Roche, Jeff. *Restructured Resistance: The Sibley Commission and the Politics of Desegregation in Georgia.* Athens: University of Georgia Press, 1998.

Ward, Jason Morgan. *Defending White Democracy: The Making of a Segregationist Movement and the Remaking of Racial Politics, 1936–1965.*

Chapel Hill: University of North Carolina Press, 2011.
Welner, Kevin G. *NeoVouchers: The Emergence of Tuition Tax Credits for Private Schooling.* Lanham, MD: Rowman & Littlefield, 2008.
White, John W. *"Managed Compliance: White Resistance and Desegregation in South Carolina, 1950–1970. "* PhD diss., University of Florida, 2006.
Williams, Robin M., and Margaret W. Ryan, eds. *Schools in Transition: Community Experiences in Desegregation.* Chapel Hill: University of North Carolina Press, 1954.
Woodley, Ken. *The Road to Healing: A Civil Rights Reparations Story in Prince Edward County, Virginia.* Montgomery: NewSouth Books, 2019.

WEB

Cierniak, Katherine, Molly Stewart, and Anne-Maree Ruddy. "Mapping the Growth of Statewide Voucher Programs in the United States." Bloomington, IN: Center for Evaluation & Education Policy, March 2015. http://ceep.indiana.edu/pdf/Statewide_Vouchers_CEEP_EPB.pdf.
Erwin, Benjamin. "Interactive Guide to School Choice Laws." National Conference of State Legislatures. April 18, 2019. http://www.ncsl.org/research/education/interactive-guide-to-school-choice.aspx#/.
Ford, Chris, Stephenie Johnson, and Lisette Partelow. "The Racist Origins of Private School Vouchers." Washington, DC: Center for American Progress, July 12, 2017. https://cdn.americanprogress.org/content/uploads/2017/07/12184850/VoucherSegregation-brief2.pdf.
"NEPC Resources on Vouchers." National Education Policy Center. Accessed April 26, 2019. https://nepc.colorado.edu/topic/vouchers.
Potter, Halley. "Do Private School Vouchers Pose a Threat to Integration?" Washington, DC: Century Foundation, March 21, 2017. https://s3-us-west-2.amazonaws.com/production.tcf.org/app/uploads/2017/03/22102646/do-private-school-vouchers-pose-a-threat-to-integration.pdf.
Reardon, Sean F., and John T. Yun. "Private School Racial Enrollments and Segregation." Cambridge, MA: Civil Rights Project, June 26, 2002. https://civilrightsproject.ucla.edu/research/k-12-education/integration-and-diversity/private-school-racial-enrollments-and-segregation/Private_Schools.pdf.
"School Desegregation in the Southern and Border States." Furman

University Digital Collections Center (Greenville, South Carolina). Accessed April 4, 2019. https://cdm16821.contentdm.oclc.org/digital/collection/p16821coll22/search.

"Status and Trends in the Education of Racial and Ethnic Groups." U.S. Department of Education, National Center for Education Statistics. Accessed March 28, 2019. https://nces.ed.gov/programs/raceindicators/.

Suitts, Steve. "A New Majority Update: Low Income Students in the South and Nation." Atlanta, GA: Southern Education Foundation, October 2013. https://www.southerneducation.org/publications/newmajorityupdate/.

"Timeline: Landmark Desegregation Cases." *Education Week*, May 13, 2014. https://www.edweek.org/ew/section/multimedia/landmark-desegregation-cases.html.

Notes

1   "Interactive Guide to School Choice Laws" National Conference of State Legislatures, June 15, 2017, http://www.ncsl.org/research/education/interactive-guide-to-school-choice.aspx; "School Choice in America," EdChoice, last modified April 9, 2019, https://www.edchoice.org/school-choice/school-choice-in-america/. Twelve of the twenty-six states with voucher programs using direct appropriations, indirect tax credits, or tax savings education accounts are in the South: Alabama, Arkansas, Florida, Georgia, Louisiana, Maryland, Mississippi, Oklahoma, North Carolina, South Carolina, Tennessee, and Virginia. State programs vary in form and scope, but some, like Georgia, permit state tax dollars to be diverted for home-schooling. All charts and maps with labels indicating "South" in this article refer to a fifteen-state South, which includes the twelve states listed above as well as Kentucky, Texas, and West Virginia.

2   *School Choice Guidebook 2017–2018* (Washington, DC: American Federation for Children Growth Fund, 2018), 7–9, https://www.federationforchildren.org/wp-content/uploads/2018/10/AFC_School_Choice_Guidebook_2017-18_10.3.pdf; "2016 Public Elementary-Secondary Education Finance Data," Annual Survey of School System Finances, US Census, last modified May 17, 2018, https://www.census.gov/data/tables/2016/econ/school-finances/secondary-education-finance.html.

3   "Trump's Speech to Congress: Video and Transcript," *New York Times*, February 28, 2017, https://www.nytimes.com/2017/02/28/us/politics/trump-congress-video-transcript.html. During his speech, the President also introduced an African American student who had received a tax credit voucher.

4   Jane Mayer, "Betsy DeVos, Trump's Big-Donor Education Secretary," *New Yorker*, November 23, 2016, https://www.newyorker.com/news/news-desk/betsy-devos-trumps-big-donor-education-secretary; Emma Brown, "DeVos Promises 'the Most Ambitious Expansion of Education Choice in Our Nation's History'—but Offers No Details," *Washington Post*, May 22, 2017, https://www.washingtonpost.com/local/education/betsy-devos-promises-the-most-ambitious-expansion-of-education-choice-in-our-nations-history--but-offers-no-details/2017/05/22/ae90f55e-3f03-11e7-8c25-44d09ff5a4a8_story.html; Valerie Strauss, Danielle Douglas-Gabriel, and Moriah Balingit, "DeVos Seeks Cuts from Education Department to Support School Choice," *Washington Post*, February 13, 2018, https://www.washingtonpost.com/

news/education/wp/2018/02/12/devos-seeks-massive-cuts-from-education-department-to-support-school-choice; Laura Meckler, "The Education of Betsy DeVos: Why Her School Choice Agenda Has Not Advanced," *Washington Post*, September 4, 2018, https://www.washingtonpost.com/local/education/the-education-of-betsy-devos-why-her-school-choice-agenda-has-crashed/2018/09/04/c21119b8-9666-11e8-810c-5fa705927d54_story.html; US Department of Education, "Fiscal Year 2019 Budget: Summary and Background Information, last modified February 12, 2018, https://www2.ed.gov/about/overview/budget/budget19/summary/19summary.pdf.

5   Romney for President, "A Chance for Every Child: Mitt Romney's Plan for Restoring the Promise of American Education," May 23, 2012, Chesapeake Digital Preservation Group, Georgetown Law Library, https://web.archive.org/web/20180624193755/http:/cdm16064.contentdm.oclc.org/cdm/ref/collection/p266901coll4/id/3980. The white paper was endorsed in a foreword by former Florida governor Jeb Bush.

6   Motoko Rich, "Bill to Offer an Option to Give Vouchers," *New York Times*, January 27, 2014, https://www.nytimes.com/2014/01/28/education/senator-to-propose-school-vouchers-program.html; American Enterprise Institute, "Senators Lamar Alexander and Tim Scott Unveil Ambitious Proposal to Expand School Choice," January 28, 2014, http://www.aei.org/events/senators-lamar-alexander-and-tim-scott-unveil-ambitious-proposals-to-expand-school-choice/; Lamar Alexander, "Weekly Column by Lamar Alexander: The 'Scholarship for Kids' Act," Weekly Columns, Lamar Alexander: United States Senator for Tennessee, February 18, 2014, https://www.alexander.senate.gov/public/index.cfm/2014/2/weekly-column-by-lamar-alexander-the-scholarships-for-kids-act; See also CHOICE Act, S. 1909, 113th Cong. (2014) and Scholarships for Kids Act, S. 1968, 115th Cong. (2017).

7   Ron Lieber, "Yes, You Really Can Pay for Private School With 529 Plans Now," *New York Times*, December 21, 2017, https://www.nytimes.com/2017/12/21/your-money/529-plans-taxes-private-school.html. This federal change supplements the Coverdell Education Savings Accounts passed first in the Clinton administration and expanded during the George W. Bush administration. It allows a limited use of federal tax dollars to support attendance at private elementary and secondary schools. See Coverdell Education Savings Accounts, 26 U.S.C. ¬ß 530 (2006). Most private schools, as nonprofit organizations, receive contributions that are deductible for donors from federal income taxes. They also are exempt from income taxes and often local property taxes.

8   "529 Plan Data," College Savings Plan Network, June 30, 2018, http://www.collegesavings.org/wp-content/uploads/2018/10/June-2018-529-plan-data-10.15.18.pdf.

9   "Public Charter School Enrollment," *The Condition of Education 2018*,

National Center for Education Statistics, 2018, https://nces.ed.gov/programs/coe/pdf/coe_cgb.pdf; "Private School Enrollment," *The Condition of Education 2018*, National Center for Education Statistics, 2018, https://nces.ed.gov/programs/coe/pdf/coe_cgc.pdf. Also, see Peter Bergman and Isaac McFarlin Jr., "Education for All? A Nationwide Audit Study of Schools of Choice" (working paper 25396, National Bureau of Economic Research, December 2018).

10   John Kirtley, "Facing a Harsh Truth When Fighting for a Bipartisan Cause," RedefinED, May 20, 2011, https://www.redefinedonline.org/2011/05/facing-a-harsh-truth-when-fighting-for-a-bipartisan-cause/; Katie Nielsen, "How School Choice Helps Advance Martin Luther King's Legacy," My Heritage, Heritage Foundation, August 28, 2013, https://www.myheritage.org/news/how-school-choice-helps-advance-martin-luther-kings-legacy/.

11   Kristen M. Clark, "Thousands Rally in Support of Program Opposed by Union," *Miami Herald*, January 19, 2016, www.miamiherald.com/news/politics-government/state-politics/article55454785.html. Martin Luther King III attended and graduated from the private Galloway School, created in Atlanta in 1969. Earlier, his parents attempted to enter him into another Atlanta private school when he reached school age in the 1960s, after they were misinformed by an Episcopal priest that the all-white, private Lovett School would accept their son. Their written application for his admission was denied without reference to a reason, although the chairman of the school board later stated that he believed that both the "negro and the white man has some individual rights." "Diversity and Inclusion at Galloway," The Galloway School, accessed March 27, 2019, https://www.gallowayschool.org/community-life/diversity-inclusion; Kevin M. Kruse, *White Flight: Atlanta and the Making of Modern Conservatism* (Princeton, NJ: Princeton University Press, 2005), 175–177.

12   See C. Vann Woodward, *The Strange Career of Jim Crow* (New York: Oxford University Press, 1966); Pauli Murray, *States' Laws on Race and Color* (Cincinnati, OH: Women's Division of Christian Service of the Methodist Church, 1951), 3–20; J. Mills Thornton III, "Segregation and the City: White Supremacy in Alabama in the Mid-Twentieth Century," in *Fog of War: The Second World War and the Civil Rights Movement*, eds. Kevin M. Kruse and Stephen Tuck (New York: Oxford University Press, 2012), 52–55.

13   Walter Spearman and Sylvan Meyer, *Racial Crisis and the Press* (Atlanta, GA: Southern Regional Council, 1960), 47.

14   See Gene Roberts and Hank Klibanoff, *The Race Beat: The Press, the Civil Rights Struggle, and the Awakening of a Nation* (New York: Random House, 2006), 56, 301–325, 376–379.

15   See Dan T. Carter, *The Politics of Rage: George Wallace, the Origins of the*

New Conservatism, and the Transformation of American Politics (New York: Simon & Schuster, 1995), 451–468. Wallace prompted controversies over "free speech" rights on college campuses into the 1970s and remains today a popular reference for personifying the Southern segregationist. See Peter Salovey, "Free Speech, Personified," *New York Times*, November 26, 2017, https://www.nytimes.com/2017/11/26/opinion/free-speech-yale-civil-rights.html.

16 *Brown v. Board of Education of Topeka*, 347 U.S. 483 (1954).

17 Spearman and Meyer, *Racial Crisis and the Press*, 19, 25, 46–48, 52. Meyer explains how "mix" was a "scare word." Justin Driver, "Supremacies and the Southern Manifesto," *Texas Law Review* 92 (2014): 1082, https://chicagounbound.uchicago.edu/journal_articles/4043/.

18 David L. Chappell, "The Divided Mind of Southern Segregationists," *Georgia Historical Quarterly* 82, no. 1 (Spring 1998): 45–72; James Graham Cook, *The Segregationists* (New York: Appleton-Century-Crofts, 1962), 5–6; Clive Webb, ed., *Massive Resistance: Southern Opposition to the Second Reconstruction* (New York: Oxford University Press, 2005), 8–9. The different factors influencing all policy issues, including race, in the segregated South were detailed by state in V. O. Key Jr., *Southern Politics in State and Nation* (New York: Alfred A. Knopf, 1949). These different factors also were evident in Southern white attitudes toward African American education. See Gunnar Myrdal, *An American Dilemma: The Negro Problem and Modern Democracy* (New York: Harper and Brothers, 1944), 893–900. For an example of class divisions during desegregation, see Karen Anderson, "The Little Rock School Desegregation Crisis: Moderation and Social Conflict," *Journal of Southern History* 70, no. 3 (August 2004): 603–636.

19 Driver, "Supremacies and the Southern Manifesto," 1079.

20 This study is, of course, not the first essay to explore the Southern segregationist origins of private school vouchers for elementary and secondary schools. See, for example, Chris Ford, Stephenie Johnson, and Lisette Partelow, *The Racist Origins of Private School Vouchers* (Washington, DC: Center for American Progress, July 12, 2017), https://www.americanprogress.org/issues/education-k-12/reports/2017/07/12/435629/racist-origins-private-school-vouchers/, and Mark A. Gooden, Huriya Jabbar, and Mario S. Torres Jr., "Race and School Vouchers: Legal, Historical, and Political Contexts," *Peabody Journal of Education* 91, no. 4 (2016): 522–536.

21 Dick M. Carpenter II and Krista Kafer, "A History of Private School Choice," *Peabody Journal of Education* 87, no. 3 (2012): 336–338. For a review of the Court's decisions leading up to *Brown*, see Richard Kluger, *Simple Justice: The History of Brown v. Board of Education and Black America's Struggle for Equality* (New York: Alfred A. Knopf, 1976), 256–284; Sam P. Wiggins,

Higher Education in the South (Berkeley, CA: McCutchan Pub. Corp., 1966), 169. There is an earlier history of school choice in the United States, when Catholic schools competed with public schools, often decidedly Protestant in nature, that carried forward into the twentieth century. See Robert N. Gross, *Public vs. Private: The Early History of School Choice in America* (New York: Oxford University Press, 2018). Yet, Gross largely ignores the pivotal period of Reconstruction when African American representatives helped to write new Southern state constitutions mandating public schools as an essential duty of state governments. W. E. B. Du Bois, *Black Reconstruction in America, 1860–1880* (New York: MacMillan, 1992), 637–669.

22   See Norman Dorsen, "Racial Discrimination in 'Private' Schools," *William & Mary Law Review* 9, no. 1 (1967): 46, https://scholarship.law.wm.edu/wmlr/vol9/iss1/4/.

23   Reaction to *Brown* was comparatively muted outside the South since the Supreme Court struck down only school segregation established by law, and most segregation laws were in Southern states. There was widespread *de facto* school segregation outside the South but only in a relatively few places did the law erect a dual system of publicly financed education based on race or ethnicity. See Murray, *States' Laws on Race and Color;* Robin M. Williams Jr. and Margaret W. Ryan, eds., *Schools in Transition: Community Experiences in Desegregation* (Chapel Hill: University of North Carolina Press, 1954); Will Maslow, "De Facto Public School Segregation," *Villanova Law Review* 6, no. 3 (1961), https://digitalcommons.law.villanova.edu/vlr/vol6/iss3/2/.

24   W. D. Workman Jr., "The Deep South," in *With All Deliberate Speed: Segregation-Desegregation in Southern Schools,* ed. Don Shoemaker (New York: Harper and Brothers, 1957), 97–100; House Resolution No. 225, *Acts and Resolutions of the General Assembly of the State of Georgia,* 1953, November–December Session, vol. 2, 241; Molly Townes O'Brien, "Private School Tuition Vouchers and the Realities of Racial Politics," *Tennessee Law Review* 64, no. 2 (1997): 359–407. Louisiana adopted a constitutional amendment in 1954 affirming its police powers to prevent desegregation of public schools, and this amendment apparently was interpreted to provide the state legislature will the power to fund private schools. See *Poindexter v. Louisiana Financial Assistance Commission,* 275 F. Supp. 833 (1967).

25   Tom Flake, "475 Legislative Actions Pertain to Race, Schools," *Southern School News,* May 1964, B-1.

26   For a full treatment of the methods and strategies of resistance, including diverting public resources to private schools, see Thomas V. O'Brien, *The Politics of Race and Schooling: Public Education in Georgia, 1900–1961* (Lanham, MD: Lexington Books, 1999), 99–198.

27   Arthur Larentz Carlson, "With All Deliberate Speed: The Pearsall Plan and

School Desegregation in North Carolina, 1954–1966" (master's thesis, East Carolina University, 2011); Jim Leeson, "Private Schools Continue to Increase in the South," *Southern Education Report* 2 (November 1966): 22–25; Walter F. Murphy, "Private Education with Public Funds," *Journal of Politics* 20, no. 4 (November 1954): 636–637; Lester Tanzer, "Private School Push: Integration of Virginia Public Schools Spurs Growth of Private Units," *Wall Street Journal*, February 6, 1959; Neil R. McMillen, *The Citizens' Council: Organized Resistance to the Second Reconstruction, 1954–64* (Urbana: University of Illinois Press, 1971), 297–304; Mary Ellen Goodman, *Sanctuaries for Tradition: Virginia's New Private Schools* (Atlanta, GA: Southern Regional Council, 1961).

28   Clay Gowran, "Faubus Tells 'Legal Plan' To Segregate," *Chicago Daily Tribune,* September 19, 1958; *Journal of the House of Representatives*, State of Georgia, Regular Session, 1959, 80; "'Resistance' Laws Urged in Georgia: Governor Offers 6 Measures Designed to Strengthen Segregated Schools," *New York Times,* January 16, 1959; "Georgia Asked To Strengthen Segregation: Six Bills Offered by Governor," *Chicago Daily Tribune,* January 16, 1959.

29   "May Veto Plan To Sell Segregation," *Daily Defender,* June 8, 1959; Lester Tanzer, "Private School Push: Integration of Virginia Public Schools Spurs Growth of Private Units Norfolk Academy, Others Will Expand; State Aids Shift, Authorizes Tuition Grants A Pattern for Solid South? Private School Push: Integration in Virginia Spurs Growth of Units," *Wall Street Journal,* February 6, 1959; Raymond Moley, "Children Are the Real Victims of the School Integration War," *Los Angeles Times,* May 18, 1961; Jon Nordheimer, "Integration Raises the Issue of Coeducation in South," *New York Times,* June 4, 1970.

30   Boutwell's reputation as a moderate grew larger after he ran against and defeated Birmingham Police Commissioner Eugene "Bull" Connor in a race for mayor. "Albert Boutwell Lieutenant Governor: 1959–1963," Alabama Department of Archives and History, last modified August 20, 2009, http://www.archives.state.al.us/conoff/Boutwell.html.

31   Edward R. Crowther, "Alabama's Fight to Maintain Segregated Schools," *Alabama Review* 43 (1990): 209–210; Thomas Jasper Gilliam Sr., "The Second Folsom Administration: The Destruction of Alabama Liberalism" (PhD diss., Auburn University, 1975), 107, 116, 194, 384. Johnston played a behind-the-scenes role in Alabama on racial matters. As a life-long white supremacist, he worked with state political and business leaders after both world wars in developing laws and strategies to thwart the expectations and aspirations of returning black soldiers. Yet after managing a presidential primary campaign, Johnston nominated Alabama senator Oscar W. Underwood as the anti-Klan candidate for president at the Democratic National Convention of 1924.

John W. Davis, who later argued before the US Supreme Court on behalf of Southern states in *Brown*, won the nomination over Underwood after an unprecedented number of ballots. Johnston was a formidable and talented legal opponent. Steve Suitts, *Hugo Black of Alabama* (Montgomery, AL: NewSouth Books, 2005), 235–236, 462–472; "Roosevelt Stand on Policies Asked; Forney Johnston Urges Chamber to Seek Clarification of President's Objectives," *New York Times*, May 1, 1935; "Graves Is Accused in Scottsboro Case," *New York Times*, December 25, 1938; John Temple Graves, "The Wage-War Between the States," *Nation's Business*, June 1934, 42; Frank W. Boykin to Mrs. Forney Johnston, June 7, 1962, Frank W. Boykin Papers, Alabama Department of Archives and History.

32 *Report of Alabama Interim Legislative Committee on Segregation in the Public Schools*, prepared by the Alabama Legislature Interim Committee on Segregation in the Public Schools (Alabama, 1954), Digital Collections, Birmingham Public Library, http://bplonline.cdmhost.com/digital/collection/p4017coll8/id/14971/rec/1; Jay Murphy, "Can Public Schools Be 'Private?'" *Alabama Law Review* 7, no. 1 (1954): 64–73; "Alabama," *Southern School News*, October 1, 1954.

33 Fred Taylor, "'Freedom of Choice' Bill Seeks School Solution in Alabama," *Atlanta Journal-Constitution*, February 12, 1956; Fred Taylor, "3-School System Amendment Expected to Pass in Alabama," *Atlanta Journal-Constitution*, August 26, 1956; Crowther, "Alabama's Fight," 214; "Georgia," *Southern School News*, September 3, 1954; Carter, *The Politics of Rage*, 83.

34 *Pierce v. Society of Sisters*, 268 U.S. 510 (1925).

35 Joseph F. Johnston, "Schools, the Supreme Court, and the States' Power To Direct the Removal of Gunpowder," *Alabama Lawyer* 17, no. 3 (1956): 3–10.

36 Fred Taylor, "School Segregation Problem No. 1 on Ala. Legislature List: Measures Proposing Varied Plans Readied for Extra Session Call," *Atlanta Journal-Constitution*, January 2, 1955; "Alabama," *Southern School News*, February 3, 1955, 3; J. Tyra Harris, "Alabama Reaction to the Brown Decision, 1954–1956: A Case Study in Early Massive Resistance" (PhD diss., Middle Tennessee State University, 1978), 208–209.

37 Lucy was summarily suspended "for her own safety" after a series of riotous events on campus following her attendance. Charles Morgan Jr., *A Time To Speak* (New York: Harper and Row, 1964), 37–39. At a 2017 university ceremony dedicating a historical marker in her honor, Lucy recalled that whites had chanted: "Hey, Hey, Ho! Where in the Hell did the nigger go?" See Jessa Reid Bolling and Rebecca Griesbach, "Autherine Lucy Foster Memorialized with Historical Marker," *The Crimson White*, September 18, 2017, 3, http://now.dirxion.com/Crimson_White/library/Crimson_White_09_18_2017.

pdf; AL.com, "Autherine Lucy Foster Monument Unveiled," YouTube video, 1:56, September 17, 2017, https://youtu.be/6jriSBIwSHg.

38   Harris, "Alabama Reaction to the Brown Decision," 226–229, 241–249; Gilliam Sr., "The Second Folsom Administration," 316–321, 374–384, 423–436; Joseph M. Bagley, "School Desegregation, Law and Order, and Litigating Social Justice in Alabama, 1954–1973" (PhD diss., Georgia State University, 2013), 104–105; *Shuttlesworth v. Birmingham Board of Education*, 162 F. Supp. 372 (1958) affirmed by *Shuttlesworth v. Board of Education*, 358 U.S. 101 (1958); "Alabama: Governor Renews Vow to Resist Integration," *Southern School News*, February 1961, 14; Warren Trest, *Nobody But the People: The Life and Times of Alabama's Youngest Governor* (Montgomery, AL: NewSouth Books, 2008), 260, 303–306; William Warren Rogers et al., *Alabama: A History of a Deep South State* (Tuscaloosa: University of Alabama Press, 1994), 547–548.

39   Carter, *The Politics of Rage*, 96–109.

40   George C. Wallace, "The Inaugural Address of Governor George C. Wallace," January 14, 1963, Alabama Textual Materials Collections, Alabama Department of Archives and History, transcript, http://digital.archives.alabama.gov/cdm/ref/collection/voices/id/2952.

41   Carter, *The Politics of Rage*, 133–293; Stephan Lesher, *George Wallace: American Populist* (Boston, MA: Addison Wesley, 1994), 244–253; *Lee v. Macon County Board of Education*, 267 F. Supp. 458 (1967); Allen Tullos, *Alabama Getaway: The Political Imaginary and the Heart of Dixie* (Athens: University of Georgia Press, 2011), 233–241.

42   "Mississippi," *Southern School News*, September 3, 1954; Charles C. Bolton, *The Hardest Deal of All: The Battle Over School Integration in Mississippi* (Jackson: University Press of Mississippi, 2005), 65–68, 75–88; McMillen, *The Citizens' Council*, 15–32, 360–361; John Dittmer, *Local People: The Struggle for Civil Rights in Mississippi* (Urbana: University of Illinois Press, 1994), 45–72; Charles M. Payne, *I've Got the Light of Freedom: The Organizing Tradition and the Mississippi Freedom Struggle* (Berkeley: University of California Press, 1995), 34–37.

43   Michael J. Klarman, "Why Massive Resistance?" in *Massive Resistance: Southern Opposition to the Second Reconstruction*, ed. Clive Webb (New York: Oxford University Press, 2005), 27.

44   Dennis J. Mitchell, *Mississippi Liberal: A Biography of Frank E. Smith* (Jackson: University Press of Mississippi, 2001), 130; Constance Curry, "A Right to Be There," *Southern Changes* 14, no. 1 (1992): 18–25, http://southernchanges. digitalscholarship.emory.edu/sc14-3_1204/sc14-3_005/; Winson Hudson and Connie Curry, *Mississippi Harmony: Memoirs of a Freedom Fighter* (New York: Palgrave MacMillan, 2002), 47–73; Marin Noel and Roderick Wright,

"Mrs. Murtis Powell: On the Front Lines of Battle," in *Minds Stayed on Freedom: The Civil Rights Struggle in the Rural South, an Oral History*, ed. Youth of the Rural Organizing and Cultural Center (Boulder, CO: Westview Press, 1991), 110–115.

45 *Survey of School Desegregation in the Southern and Border States, 1965–1966* (Washington, DC: United States Commission on Civil Rights, 1966), 33–42, https://www2.law.umaryland.edu/marshall/usccr/documents/cr12sch611. pdf; *Alexander v. Holmes County Board of Education*, 396 US 19 (1969); McMillen, *The Citizens' Council*, 302; Bolton, *The Hardest Deal of All*, 169–186.

46 Jim Carl, *Freedom of Choice: Vouchers in American Education* (Santa Barbara, CA: Praeger, 2011), 26–28; "Louisiana," *Southern School News*, September 3, 1954, 13; Charles A. Reynard, "Legislation Affecting Segregation," *Louisiana Law Review* 17 (1956–57): 104–114. For a brief time, Rainach later became head of the Louisiana Sovereignty Commission, the primary state apparatus to spy on and harass civil rights activists and supporters. Carl, *Freedom of Choice*, 37, 46.

47 Carl, *Freedom of Choice*, 29–32; "Supreme Court Approves Invalidation of Louisiana's Pupil Placement Law," *Southern School News*, July 1957, 7. In New Orleans, the Catholic schools were uniquely more willing to integrate sooner than the public schools. As early as 1956, the Archbishop publicly declared that segregation was morally wrong.

48 Adam Fairclough, *Race and Democracy: The Civil Rights Struggle in Louisiana, 1915–1972* (Athens: University of Georgia Press, 1995), 247.

49 Carl, *Freedom of Choice*, 47–48; "State Again Fails To Get Control of Orleans Schools," *Southern School News*, February 1961, 6.

50 Carl, *Freedom of Choice*, 48–53; "Louisiana Legislators Go Home; Teachers Miss Pay," *Southern School News*, January 1961, 1, 8–11; *Poindexter*, 275 F. Supp. 833.

51 John E. Batchelor, *Race and Education in North Carolina: From Segregation to Desegregation* (Baton Rouge: Louisiana State University Press, 2015), 32–42; Carlson, "With All Deliberate Speed," 55–59.

52 Batchelor, *Race and Education*, 36–40.

53 Batchelor, *Race and Education*, 76–110; Carlson, "With All Deliberate Speed," 72; Douglas Martin, "Julius Chambers, a Fighter for Civil Rights, Dies at 76," *New York Times*, August 6, 2013, https://www.nytimes.com/2013/08/07/us/julius-chambers-a-fighter-for-civil-rights-dies-at-76.html; "*Hawkins v. North Carolina State Board of Education*," *Race Relations Law Reporter* 11 (1966): 745, 747.

54 Joseph J. Thorndike, "'The Sometimes Sordid Level of Race and Segregation': James J. Kilpatrick and the Virginia Campaign against Brown," in *The*

Moderates' Dilemma: Massive Resistance to School Desegregation in Virginia, eds. Matthew D. Lassiter and Andrew B. Lewis (Charlottesville: University Press of Virginia, 1998), 70.

55 Carl W. Tobias, "Public School Desegregation in Virginia During the Post-Brown Decade," *William & Mary Law Review* 37 (1996): 1269–1271.

56 Commission on Public Education, "Report of the Commission to the Governor of Virginia" (Richmond, 1959). This report is also referred to as the Perrow Report in reference to the chairman of the Commission, Mosby G. Perrow Jr.

57 "Report of the Commission to the Governor of Virginia," 21–25; "Virginia: State Commission Draws Up New Legislative Proposals," *Southern School News*, April 1959, 16; George M. Cochran, "Virginia Facing Reality: The 1959 Perrow Commission," Augusta Historical Bulletin 42 (2006), http://mlkcommission.dls.virginia.gov/va_school_closings/pdfs/Cochrane%20Augusta%20Historical%20Bulletin.pdf; *Griffin v. School Board of Prince Edward County*, 377 U.S. 218 (1964) at 233.

58 John W. White, "Managed Compliance: White Resistance and Desegregation in South Carolina, 1950–1970" (PhD diss., University of Florida, 2006), 152.

59 Stephen Harold Lowe, "'The Magnificent Fight': Civil Rights Litigation in South Carolina Federal Courts, 1940–1970" (PhD diss., University of Michigan, 1999), 193–201; White, "Managed Compliance," 43–61; "South Carolina," *Southern School News*, September 3, 1954, 12.

60 White, "Managed Compliance," 151–153. "Academic standards" without any reference to race or skin color also were used to assure that African American teachers did not receive equal pay with white teachers, despite a federal court order to equalize teachers' salaries. Also see R. Scott Baker, "Testing Equality: The National Teacher Examination and the NAACP's Legal Campaign to Equalize Teachers' Salaries in the South 1936–63," *History of Education Quarterly* 35, no. 1 (1995): 49–64 and R. Scott Baker, "The Paradoxes of Desegregation: Race, Class, and Education, 1935–1975," *American Journal of Education* 109, no. 3 (May 2001): 320–343. The Gressette Committee also attempted to convince the NAACP lawyers that geography, not the state government, was responsible for school segregation. See Maxie Myron Cox Jr., "1963—the Year of Decision: Desegregation in South Carolina" (PhD diss., University of South Carolina, 1996), 166.

61 "South Carolina," *Southern School News*, January 6, 1955, 14.

62 White, "Managed Compliance," 166–265.

63 "South Carolina," *Southern School News*, February 3, 1955, 3; "South Carolina," *Southern School News*, March 3, 1955, 14; "South Carolina," *Southern School News*, July 1955, 4. Even bills proposing confrontational tactics, such

as closing public schools, often did not mention race. For example, a bill in 1955 proposed to close any public school where a student was admitted by court order. See "South Carolina," *Southern School News*, May 4, 1955, 6. In 1960, on advice of the Gressette Committee, the legislature removed the phrase "for racially segregated schools only" from its appropriations bill. See Cox Jr., "1963—the Year of Decision," 15.

64 "Clemson College Admits Negro in State's First Desegregation," *Southern School News*, February 1963, 1; Interview with Harvey B. Gantt by William R. Ferris, September 28, 2015, C-0367, Southern Oral History Program Collection #4007, Southern Historical Collection, Wilson Library, University of North Carolina at Chapel Hill, https://dc.lib.unc.edu/cdm/compoundobject/collection/sohp/id/27218/rec/2.

65 "Clemson College Admits Negro on Order of Appellate Court," *Southern School News*, February 1963, 8–9.

66 White, "Managed Compliance," 390–391; *Brown v. South Carolina State Board of Education*, 296 F. Supp. 199 (1968).

67 O'Brien, "Private School Vouchers and the Reality of Racial Politics," 79–92.

68 O'Brien, 105–108; "Georgia Attorney General Says Supreme Court Will Mix Schools," *Chicago Defender*, October 31, 1953, 5; *Acts and Resolutions of the General Assembly of the State of Georgia, 1956*, vol. 1, 10–11, 13–15. These laws followed the passage of a 1955 law mandating that in Georgia "no State or local funds shall be in any manner appropriated or expended for public school purposes except for schools in which the white and colored races are separately educated." See *Acts and Resolutions of the General Assembly of the State of Georgia, 1955*, vol. 1, 174–176.

69 *Acts and Resolutions of the General Assembly of the State of Georgia, 1959*, vol. 1, 7, 15, 157; "Georgia: Teachers Endorse Separate-But-Equal; Decision Awaited In State Test Case," *Southern School News*, April 1959, 7.

70 "Motion to Dismiss Is Overruled," *Atlanta Daily World*, December 16, 1958.

71 O'Brien, "Private School Vouchers and the Reality of Racial Politics," 174.

72 O'Brien, 171–181; *Acts and Resolutions of the General Assembly of the State of Georgia, 1960*, vol. 1, 1187; Jeff Roche, *Restructured Resistance: The Sibley Commission and the Politics of Desegregation in Georgia* (Athens: University of Georgia Press, 1998), 163–172; "Here's Text of Majority Report by Sibley Committee," *Atlanta Constitution*, April 29, 1960; "Text of Minority Report," *Atlanta Constitution*, April 29, 1960; Paul Delaney, "Judge Hooper to Study Sibley Report Monday," *Atlanta Daily World*, May 8, 1960.

73 Matthew D. Lassiter, *The Silent Majority: Suburban Politics in the Sunbelt South* (Princeton, NJ: Princeton University Press, 2006), 87–89.

74 O'Brien, "Private School Vouchers and the Reality of Racial Politics," 189–191, 199–201; "Gov. Ernest Vandiver Asks 4-Point Child Protection

Defense Package," *Atlanta Daily World,* January 19, 1961; "U.S. Judge Rejects Contentions of Georgia Officials," *Southern School News,* February 1961, 8; *Acts and Resolutions of the General Assembly of the State of Georgia, 1961,* vol. 1, 35.

75 Kruse, *White Flight,* 150–156.

76 Lassiter, *The Silent Majority,* 104–105.

77 Bruce Galphin, "40 Negro Students File Appeals for Transfers," *Atlanta Constitution,* June 14, 1961; Bruce Galphin, "38 Negroes, White Girl Lose Transfer Appeals," *Atlanta Constitution,* July 7, 1961; Tomoko Brown-Nagin, *Courage to Dissent: Atlanta and the Long History of the Civil Rights Movement* (New York: Oxford University Press, 2011), 307.

78 Kruse, *White Flight,* 9–17, 161–177, 234–235; John H. Britton, "Fear of Increase in Taxes Is Blamed for Bond Measure Defeat: Negro Votes Favored Most Bond Proposals," *Atlanta Daily World,* August 4, 1962; "$206,640 Granted Students to Attend Jim Crow Schools," *Atlanta Daily World,* October 17, 1962.

79 See these federal cases: Coffey v. State Educational Finance Commission, 296 F. Supp. 1389 (S.D. Miss. 1969); Griffin v. State Board of Education, 296 F. Supp. 1178 (E.D. Va. 1969); Poindexter v. Louisiana Financial Assistance Commission, 296 F. Supp. 686 (E.D. La. 1968); Brown v. South Carolina State Board of Education, 296 F. Supp. 199 (D.S.C. 1968), *aff'd,* 393 U.S. 222 (1968); Poindexter v. Louisiana Financial Assistance Commission, 275 F. Supp. 833 (E.D. La. 1968), *aff'd,* 389 U.S. 571 (1968); Lee v. Macon County Board of Education, 267 F. Supp. 458 (M.D. Ala. 1967); Hawkins v. North Carolina State Board of Education, 11 Race Relations Law Reporter 745 (W.D.N.C. 1966); Griffin v. State Board of Education, 239 F. Supp. 560 (E.D. Va. 1965); Lee v. Macon County Board of Education, 231 F. Supp. 743 (E.D. Ala. 1964); Pettaway v. County School Board, 230 F. Supp. 480 (E.D. Va. 1964), *aff'd,* 339 F. 2d 486 (2d Cir. 1964); Hall v. St. Helena Parish School Board, 231 F. Supp. 649 (E.D. La. 1961), *aff'd,* 368 U.S. 515 (1962); Aaron v. McKinley, 173 F. Supp. 944 (E.D. Ark. 1959), *aff'd sub nom,* Faubus v. Arron, 361 U.S. 197 (1959).

80 Tom P. Brady, "Segregation and the South," October 4, 1957, Citizens' Council Collection, Archives and Special Collections, University of Mississippi Libraries; McMillen, *The Citizens' Council,* 265–266; Thomas P. Brady, interview by Orley B. Caudill, March 4, 1972, Center for Oral History and Cultural Heritage, University of Southern Mississippi Libraries. In 1962, Arnold Rose, who assisted Gunnar Myrdal, wrote a postscript in the 1962 edition of *An American Dilemma* (New York: McGraw Hill, xxxv–xxxvii) where he discussed how the initial monolithic response to *Brown* by Southern whites changed and adapted to fit the times.

81 Harry S. Ashmore, *Hearts and Minds: The Anatomy of Racism from Roosevelt to Reagan* (New York: McGraw Hill, 1982), 214.

82 Brown-Nagin, *Courage to Dissent,* 336; Donald Hollowell, conversation with the author, May 1978.

83 Brown-Nagin, 307–309.

84 Robert B. Patterson, *2nd Annual Report* (Greenwood, MS: Association of Citizens' Councils of Mississippi, August 1956), 2.

85 Driver, "Supremacies and the Southern Manifesto," 1093. While discussing the ideas and strategies voiced by Southern federal officials, Driver illuminates the components of segregationists' plans of resistance that "play a role today in maintaining the paucity of meaningful integration in the nation's public schools." See pages 1094, 1097–1099.

86 *Statistical Summary: School Segregation–Desegregation in the Southern and Border States* (Nashville, TN: Southern Education Reporting Service, 1966–67), 43.

87 Milton Friedman, "The Role of Government in Education," in *Economics and the Public Interest,* ed. Robert A. Solo (New Brunswick, NJ: Rutgers University Press, 1955), 123–144. Friedman was awarded the Nobel Prize for economics in 1976 for his work on monetary policy.

88 Friedman, "The Role of Government in Education," 129.

89 Milton Friedman, *Capitalism and Freedom* (Chicago: University of Chicago Press, 2002), 111–115; "Friedman Cautions Against Rights Bill," *Harvard Crimson,* May 5, 1964.)

90 Friedman, "The Role of Government in Education," 131, fn. 2.

91 Tom P. Brady, *Black Monday* (Winona, MS: Association of Citizens' Councils, 1954), 56; Brady, interview.

92 Johnston, "Schools, the Supreme Court, and the States' Power," 3–10.

93 James H. Hershman and the *Dictionary of Virginia Biography,* "Leon S. Dure (1907–1993)," Encyclopedia Virginia, last modified October 6, 2016, https://www.encyclopediavirginia.org/Dure_Leon_S_1907-1993; Leon Dure, "Virginia's New Freedom," *The Georgia Review* 18, no. 1 (Spring 1964): 4; Leon Dure, "The New Southern Response: Anatomy of Two New Freedoms," *The Georgia Review* 15, no. 4 (Winter 1961): 401–409, 412; James H. Hershman Jr., "Massive Resistance Meets Its Match: The Emergence of a Pro-Public School Majority," in *The Moderates' Dilemma: Massive Resistance to School Desegregation in Virginia,* eds. Matthew D. Lassiter and Andrew B. Lewis (Charlottesville: University Press of Virginia, 1998), 128. Dure seemed especially delighted that the US Supreme Court had recognized the "right of association" in a case where the Court prevented the Alabama attorney general's assault against the NAACP. See *NAACP v. Alabama ex rel. Patterson,*

357 U.S. 449 (1958). Dure was also influenced by the writings of Virgil Blum, a political scientist at Marquette University who advocated for school vouchers for private schools, including parochial schools, on a philosophy of free markets and freedom of religion. See Carl, *Freedom of Choice*, 91–92.

94 Hershman Jr., "Massive Resistance Meets Its Match," 127–130; C.F. Hicks to Leon Dure, June 22, 1961, Leon Dure Papers, University of Virginia, Charlottesville, Virginia.

95 Hershman Jr., "Massive Resistance Meets Its Match," 127–128, including fn. 52; Carl, *Freedom of Choice*, 91–92. The Georgia amendment became Section VIII of Article VIII of the Georgia Constitution and remained in the constitution until removed twenty years later as a "vestige of the past," although many in the early 1980s had no notion of what the provision represented. See Committee to Revise Article VIII, "Transcripts of Meetings," 22 May 1980, *State of Georgia Select Committee on Constitutional Revision, 1977–1981*, vol. I, 9.

96 Michael W. Fuquay, "Civil Rights and the Private School Movement in Mississippi, 1964–1971," *History of Education Quarterly* 42, no. 2 (Summer 2002): 163–164, 178–179. Parroting Friedman, right wing radio and media personalities such as Neal Boortz and Sean Hannity have hammered for years at "government schools." Neal Boortz, "Government Idiocy in Action at Schools," *Atlanta Journal-Constitution*, December 8, 2009, https://www.ajc.com/news/opinion/neal-boortz-government-idiocy-action-schools/mQCmFIfvMZ36Nwc2t2YoDI/; "Sean Hannity Attacks Social Security and Public Schools as Ineffective Programs Exploiting People's Fears," *Media Matters for America*, January 3, 2019, https://www.mediamatters.org/video/2019/01/03/sean-hannity-attacks-social-security-and-public-schools-ineffective-programs-exploiting-peoples/222411.

97 James Hardman Jr., "Virginia on the Cusp of Change," in *Historians in Service of a Better South*, eds. Robert J. Norrell and Andrew H. Myers (Montgomery, AL: NewSouth Books, 2017), 80.

98 *Green v. Kennedy*, 309 F. Supp. 1127 (1970) at 1130.

99 *Green*, 309 F. Supp. 1127 (1970) *aff'd sub nom*, Cannon v. Green, 398 U.S. 956 (1970); Eileen Shanahan, "Schools in South May Avoid Taxes," *New York Times*, August 3, 1967; Eileen Shanahan, "Private Schools That Bar Blacks to Lose Tax Aid," *New York Times*, July 11, 1970.

100 *Green v. Connally*, 330 F. Supp. 1150 (1971), *aff'd sub nom*, Coit v. Green, 404 U.S. 997 (1971).

101 "Proposed Rules on Tax Exemptions for Private Schools Eased by IRS," *New York Times*, February 10, 1979; *IRS Tax Exemptions and Segregated Private Schools: Hearing Before the Subcommittee on Civil and Constitutional Rights of the Committee on the Judiciary, House of Representatives*, 97th Cong., 2d

Sess. 39 (1982); also see *Tax-Exempt Status of Private Schools: Hearing Before the Subcommittee on Oversight of the Committee on Ways and Means, House of Representatives*, 99th Cong., 2d Sess. 39 (1985).

102 Julia Malone, "Those Tax Breaks for Segregated Schools Stir Storm," *Christian Science Monitor*, January 14, 1982; *Bob Jones University v. United States*, 461 U.S. 574 (1983); Strat Douthat, "Some All-White Academies Struggle," *Richmond Times-Dispatch*, March 18, 1986.

103 Terry Berkovsky, Andrew Megosh, Debra Cowen, and David Daume, "Private School Update," 2000 EO CPE Text, Internal Revenue Service, 2000, www.irs.gov/pub/irs-tege/eotopicn00.pdf. The IRS rules suggest that a school must evidence that "it currently enrolls a meaningful number of racial minority students, or that its promotional activities and recruiting efforts are reasonably designed to inform students of all racial segments in the general communities within the area of the availability of the school." But, as a matter of practice, citing language in the *Bob Jones* case that denial of tax exemptions should be made "only where there is no doubt that the organization's activities violate fundamental public policy," the IRS and the US Tax Court has denied tax status only when a school maintains total segregation. See Calhoun Academy v. Commissioner, 94 T.C. 284 (1990).

104 "Private Schools on Rise in the South," *New York Amsterdam News*, November 8, 1969; Kitty Terjen, "The Segregation Academy Movement," in *The South and Her Children: School Desegregation, 1970–1971*, ed. Robert E. Anderson Jr. (Atlanta, GA: Southern Regional Council, 1971), 69–71; "Civil Rights: Segregation: Federal Income Tax Exemptions and Deductions: The Validity of Tax Benefits to Private Segregated Schools," *Michigan Law Review* 68, no. 7 (June 1970): 1410–1414; *Alexander v. Holmes County Board of Education*, 396 U.S. 19 (1969).

105 Steve Suitts, *Race and Ethnicity in a New Era of Public Funding of Private Schools: Private School Enrollment in the South and the Nation* (Atlanta, GA: Southern Education Foundation, 2015), 7–8.

106 *Hearings on IRS Tax Exemptions and Segregated Private Schools, Before the Subcommittee on Civil and Constitutional Rights of the Committee of the Judiciary*, 97th Cong. (1982), 69; *Digest of Education Statistics, 1981* (Washington, DC: National Center for Education Statistics, 1981).

107 Jason Morgan Ward, *Defending White Democracy: The Making of a Segregationist Movement and the Remaking of Racial Politics, 1936–1965* (Chapel Hill: University of North Carolina Press, 2011), 183.

108 Terjen, "The Segregation Academy Movement," 76; Margaret Rose Gladney, "I'll Take My Stand: The Southern Segregation Academy Movement" (PhD diss., University of New Mexico, 1974), 80.

109 Kitty Griffith, "New 'Segregation Academies' Flourish in the South," *South*

Today, October 1969, 1.

110 Gladney, "I'll Take My Stand," 80.

111 Gladney, 99–126.

112 Gladney, 134–136.

113 David Nevin and Robert E. Bills, *The Schools that Fear Built: Segregationist Academies in the South* (Washington, DC: Acropolis Books, 1976), 61.

114 Nevin and Bills, 11.

115 Catherine A. Lugg, "For God and Country: Conservative Ideology and Federal School Policy during the First Term of President Ronald Reagan" (PhD diss., Pennsylvania State University, 1995), 105–111, 121.

116 Lugg, "For God and Country," 132; Julia Malone, "Drive Begins for Tuition Tax Credit: Reagan Education Secretary Argues for Private School Help," *Christian Science Monitor,* June 8, 1981; Julia Malone, "Bid to Allow Tax Credits for Private-School Tuition Awaits Next Session of Congress," *Christian Science Monitor,* November 16, 1983; David E. Rosenbaum, "Tuition Credit Seen in Reagan Plan," *New York Times,* May 27, 1985.

117 Lugg, 126–127; Engel v. Vitale, 370 U.S. 421 (1962).

118 Gladney, "I'll Take My Stand," 134.

119 Goodman, *Sanctuaries for Tradition,* 9–12; Gladney, 137.

120 Lugg, "For God and Country," 212–213; "Republican Party Platform of 1984," The American Presidency Project, accessed March 8, 2019, https://www.presidency.ucsb.edu/documents/republican-party-platform-1984; Ronald Reagan, the annual State of the Union address (speech, Washington, DC, February 4, 1986), The American Presidency Project, www.presidency.ucsb.edu/documents/address-before-joint-session-congress-the-state-the-union. The first time a national political party's platform endorsed tax credits for private schools was in 1972 at the Republican National Convention.

121 The next federal legislation providing new tax benefits to private schools was the Coverdell Education Account created in 1997 during the Clinton administration. It permits annual contributions up to $500 to earn tax-free funds to cover expenses in college or in elementary and secondary private schools. The accounts have restrictions on income and uses for K–12 private school tuition. Ironically, First Lady Hillary Clinton's first job out of law school involved investigating discriminatory practices of Southern private schools. See Amy Chozick, "How Hillary Clinton Went Undercover to Examine Race in Education," *New York Times,* December 27, 2015, www.nytimes.com/2015/12/28/us/politics/how-hillary-clinton-went-undercover-to-examine-race-in-education.html.

122 See, for example, John Egerton, "Hammond Academy: A Rebel Yell, Fading," in *Shades of Gray: Dispatches from the Modern South* (Baton Rouge: Louisiana

State University Press, 1991), 237–248.

123 See Lassiter, *The Silent Majority*, 295–324.

124 Robert W. Fairlie and Alexandra M. Resch, "Is There 'White Flight' into Private Schools? Evidence from the National Educational Longitudinal Survey," *Review of Economics and Statistics* 84 (2002): 21–33.

125 Sean F. Reardon and John T. Yun, *Private School Racial Enrollments and Segregation* (Cambridge, MA: The Civil Rights Project, Harvard University, 2002), 22, https://civilrightsproject.ucla.edu/research/k-12-education/integration-and-diversity/private-school-racial-enrollments-and-segregation/Private_Schools.pdf.

126 Reardon and Yun, *Private School Racial Enrollments and Segregation*, 22.

127 Charles T. Clotfelter, "Private Schools, Segregation, and the Southern States," *Peabody Journal of Education* 79, no. 2 (2004): 74–97.

128 Harry Brighthouse, "Egalitarian Liberals and School Choice," *Politics & Society* 24, no. 4 (1996): 457–486; James S. Coleman, "Some Points on Choice in Education," *Sociology of Education* 65, no. 4 (1992): 260–262. For a clear, deep understanding of this recent emergence of tax credits to finance enrollment at private schools, see Kevin G. Welner, *NeoVouchers: The Emergence of Tuition Tax Credits for Private Schooling* (Lanham, MD: Rowman & Littlefield, 2008).

129 *Keyes v. School Dist. No. 1, Denver*, 413 US 189 (1973), 258; Justin Driver, *The Schoolhouse Gate: Public Education, the Supreme Court, and the Battle for the American Mind* (New York: Pantheon, 2018), 278–283. As Driver notes, Justice Rehnquist as a Supreme Court law clerk had argued while *Brown* was being considered that the Court should not overrule *Plessy v. Ferguson*, 163 U.S. 537 (1896), which had sanctioned state-sponsored segregation.

130 *Allen v. Wright*, 468 US 737 (1984).

131 *Parents Involved in Community Schools v. Seattle School Dist. No. 1*, 551 US 701 (2007), 2744; Driver, *The Schoolhouse Gate*, 293–308.

132 *Arizona Christian School Tuition Organization v. Winn*, 131 U.S. 1436 (2011) at 1448. Justice Kennedy's opinion considered whether the First Amendment's clause requiring separation of church and state, by way of application to the states through the Fourteenth Amendment, prohibited providing state tax credit vouchers to religious schools.

133 Suitts, *Race and Ethnicity in a New Era of Public Funding of Private Schools*, 36–39.

134 Steve Suitts, A New *Majority: Low Income Students in the South's Public Schools* (Atlanta, GA: Southern Education Foundation, 2007), https://www.southerneducation.org/wp-content/uploads/2019/02/A-New-Majority-Report-Final.pdf; Steve Suitts, A New *Diverse Majority: Students of Color*

in the South's Public Schools (Atlanta, GA: Southern Education Foundation, 2010), https://www.southerneducation.org/wp-content/uploads/2019/02/A-New-Diverse-Majority-2010.pdf; Steve Suitts, A New *Majority: Low Income Students Now a Majority in the Nation's Public Schools* (Atlanta, GA: Southern Education Foundation, 2015), https://www.southerneducation.org/wp-content/uploads/2019/02/New-Majority-Update-Bulletin.pdf; Shaila Dewan, "Southern Schools Mark Two Majorities," *New York Times*, January 6, 2010, https://www.nytimes.com/2010/01/07/us/07south.html; Lyndsey Layton, "Majority of US Public School Students Are in Poverty," *Washington Post*, January 16, 2015, https://www.washingtonpost.com/local/education/majority-of-us-public-school-students-are-in-poverty/2015/01/15/df7171d0-9ce9-11e4-a7ee-526210d665b4_story.html.

135   Suitts, *A New Majority: Low Income Students in the South and Nation* (Atlanta, GA: Southern Education Foundation, 2013), 5–6, 15, https://www.southerneducation.org/wp-content/uploads/2019/02/New-Majority-2013.pdf; Elizabeth Kneebone, "The Changing Geography of US Poverty," The Brookings Institution, February 15, 2017, https://www.brookings.edu/testimonies/the-changing-geography-of-us-poverty/; Richard Fry, "Sharp Growth in Suburban Minority Enrollment Yields Modest Gains in School Diversity" (Washington, DC: Pew Research Center, March 31, 2009), http://www.pewhispanic.org/2009/03/31/sharp-growth-in-suburban-minority-enrollmentbryields-modest-gains-in-school-diversity/; Karen Pooley, "Segregation's New Geography: The Atlanta Metro Region, Race, and the Declining Prospects for Upward Mobility," *Southern Spaces*, April 15, 2015, https://southernspaces.org/2015/segregations-new-geography-atlanta-metro-region-race-and-declining-prospects-upward-mobility.

136   Don Boyd and Lucy Dadayan, "State and Local Governments Reshape Their Finances," *The Book of the States 2016* (Lexington, KY: The Council of State Governments, 2016), http://knowledgecenter.csg.org/kc/system/files/Boyd%20Dadayan%202016.pdf; Nikole Hannah-Jones, "The Resegregation of Jefferson County," *New York Times*, September 6, 2017, https://www.nytimes.com/2017/09/06/magazine/the-resegregation-of-jefferson-county.html; Suitts, *A New Majority: Low Income Students in the South and Nation*, 8–13.

137   Suitts, *Race and Ethnicity in a New Era of Public Funding of Private Schools,* 17, 27–29. Reardon and Yun also found that Asian students were over-represented in private schools in 1998. One other group of school-age children nationally matched their representation in private schools in 2012: students who self-identified as "of two or more races."

138   See Joyce Kuo, "Excluded, Segregated and Forgotten: A Historical View of the Discrimination of Chinese Americans in Public Schools," *Asian American*

Law Journal 5 (1998): 181–212, https://scholarship.law.berkeley.edu/cgi/viewcontent.cgi?article=1044&context=aalj; Carmen DeNavas-Walt, Bernadette D. Proctor, and Jessica C. Smith, *Income, Poverty, and Health Insurance Coverage in the United States: 2012, Current Population Reports* (Washington, DC: US Census Bureau, 2013), 5, https://www.census.gov/prod/2013pubs/p60-245.pdf; Lauren Musu-Gillette, Cristobal de Brey, Joel McFarland, William Hussar, William Sonnenberg, and Sidney Wilkinson-Flicker, *Status and Trends in the Education of Racial and Ethnic Groups 2017* (Washington, DC: US Department of Education, National Center for Education Statistics, 2017), 46–52, https://nces.ed.gov/pubs2017/2017051.pdf; Herbert J. Gans, "'Whitening' and the Changing American Racial Hierarchy," *Du Bois Review: Social Science Research on Race* 9, no. 2 (2012): 267–279.

139 Suitts, *Race and Ethnicity in a New Era of Public Funding of Private Schools,* 28. The two states with the largest percentage of Asian and Pacific Islander school-age children, Hawaii and Alaska, have an under-representation of these children in private schools—in fact, the largest gaps among the 50 states in 2012.

140 Suitts, *Race and Ethnicity in a New Era of Public Funding of Private Schools,* 40–42, 64–65. Hispanics and Native Americans have their own linked histories of discrimination in education. See Victoria-María MacDonald, "Demanding their Rights: The Latino Struggle for Educational Access and Equity," in *American Latinos and the Making of the United States: A Theme Study,* National Park Service, 2013, https://www.nps.gov/articles/latinothemeeducation.htm; Richard R. Valencia, "The Mexican American Struggle for Equal Educational Opportunity in *Mendez v. Westminster:* Helping to Pave the Way for *Brown v. Board of Education,*" *Teachers College Record* 107, no. 3 (March 2005): 389–423; David Wallace Adams, *Education for Extinction: American Indians and the Boarding School Experience, 1875–1928* (Lawrence: University Press of Kansas, 1995); Theda Perdue, "The Legacy of Indian Removal," *Journal of Southern History* 78, no. 1 (February 2012): 3–36.

141 Woodward, *The Strange Career of Jim Crow,* 107; Thomas J. Woofter, *Southern Race Progress* (Washington, DC: Public Affairs Press, 1957), 133–137. In the Jim Crow era, many Southern industrialists believed in white supremacy but did not always find absolute segregation an economic advantage for their companies. See Suitts, *Hugo Black of Alabama,* 246–250, for a précis of this condition in Birmingham.

142 Key Jr., *Southern Politics in State and Nation,* 620. Of course, attempting to vote in a Southern state's Democratic primary was dangerous or deadly for African Americans. Steven F. Lawson, *Black Ballots: Voting Rights in the South, 1944–1969* (New York: Columbia University Press, 1976), 119–121; Howell Raines, *My Soul Is Rested: Movement Days in the Deep South Remembered*

(New York: Bantam Books, 1978), 285–294; also, listen to Hank Klibanoff, *Buried Truths*, 2018, podcast, https://www.wabe.org/shows/buried-truths.

143 Michael J. Klarman, *Brown v. Board of Education and the Civil Rights Movement* (New York: Oxford University Press, 2007), 14; Charles Morgan Jr., "Segregated Justice," in *Southern Justice*, ed. Leon Friedman (New York: Random House, 1965), 159–161.

144 Hershman, "Massive Resistance Meets Its Match," 105.

145 Hershman, 104–106; Lassiter, *The Silent Majority*, 13–14, 26¬≠–29, 322–323.

146 *Brown v. Board of Education of Topeka*, 98 F. Supp. 797 (1951).

147 Murray, *State Laws on Race and Color*, 161; Institute for Social and Environmental Studies, *Kansas Statistical Abstract 1976* (Lawrence: University of Kansas, 1977), 5–9, 23, http://ipsr.ku.edu/ksdata/ksah/KSA12.pdf. There was a failed legislative effort in 1921 to change the nineteenth-century Kansas law to allow towns as small as two thousand to establish absolute segregation in schools. Thom Rosenblum, "The Segregation of Topeka's Public School System, 1879–1951," National Park Service, last modified April 10, 2015, https://www.nps.gov/brvb/learn/historyculture/topekasegregation.htm.

148 Murray, 35–36; 290–291, 144; Mary Melcher, "'This Is Not Right': Rural Arizona Women Challenge Segregation and Ethnic Division, 1925–1950," *Frontiers: A Journal of Women Studies* 20, no. 2 (1999): 198–199. Arizona did require all elementary schools to segregate by race. Melcher suggests that Arizona required school segregation due to the large number of former Southerners serving in the legislature. See Murray, 524; Reid E. Jackson, "The Development and Character of Permissive and Partly Segregated Schools," *Journal of Negro Education* 16, no. 3 (Summer 1947): 302–305.

149 Martin Luther King Jr., "Love, Law, and Civil Disobedience," *New South*, December 1961.

150 Lorri Denise Booker, "250 Protest Anti-Abortion Conference—2 Arrested; 600 Pack Omni to Hear Falwell," *Atlanta Journal-Constitution*, December 9, 1988; "Homogenized Heroes," *SRC Home Record*, Southern Regional Council, First & Second Quarters, 1989, 5. Ralph Reed, director of the Christian Coalition, continued to try to align King as the role model for conservative evangelical activists, many of whom supported public funding for private religious schools. Carter, *The Politics of Rage*, 466.

151 See Robert C. Pianta and Arya Ansan, "Does Attendance in Private Schools Predict Student Outcomes at Age 15? Evidence From a Longitudinal Study," *Educational Researcher* 47, no. 7 (2018), https://journals.sagepub.com/stoken/default+domain/XfYmtC25VddcCfbA3xiV/full; Mark Dynarski, *On Negative Effects of Vouchers* (Washington, DC: Brookings Institution, 2016), https://www.brookings.edu/research/on-negative-effects-of-vouchers/; Mark Dynarski and Austin Nichols, *More Findings about School Vouchers and Test Scores*,

and *They Are Still Negative* (Washington, DC: Brookings Institution, 2017), https://www.brookings.edu/research/more-findings-about-school-vouchers-and-test-scores-and-they-are-still-negative/; Martin Carnoy, *School Vouchers Are Not a Proven Strategy for Improving Student Achievement* (Washington, DC: Economic Policy Institute, 2017), https://www.epi.org/publication/school-vouchers-are-not-a-proven-strategy-for-improving-student-achievement/; Halley Potter, *Do Private School Vouchers Pose a Threat to Integration?* (Washington, DC: The Century Foundation, 2017), https://s3-us-west-2.amazonaws.com/production.tcf.org/app/uploads/2017/03/22102646/do-private-school-vouchers-pose-a-threat-to-integration.pdf; Kevin Carey, "Dismal Voucher Results Surprise Researchers as DeVos Era Begins," *New York Times*, February 23, 2017, https://www.nytimes.com/2017/02/23/upshot/dismal-results-from-vouchers-surprise-researchers-as-devos-era-begins.html.

152 Samuel E. Abrams, *Education and the Commercial Mindset* (Cambridge, MA: Harvard University Press, 2016), 303–307.

153 *Report of Alabama Interim Legislative Committee on Segregation in the Public Schools*, 11.

154 *Report of Alabama Interim Legislative Committee on Segregation in the Public Schools*, 7–8.

155 For video overviews of the struggles against efforts to use vouchers to privatize public education, see videos at "Vouchers and Tax Credit Scholarships in the US," Southern Education Foundation, 2015, https://www.southerneducation.org/publications/vouchersandtaxcreditscholarships/; "Advancing Public Education in the South," Southern Education Foundation, 2013, https://www.youtube.com/watch?v=dBo4HwZ_8v8.

156 For example, Jill Lepore writes that, because of the Supreme Court decision in *Coit v. Green* in 1971, "private religious schools no longer provided a refuge for whites opposed to integration." See Jill Lepore, *These Truths: A History of the United States* (New York: W.W. Norton, 2018), 663. There is no basis in fact for such a conclusion.

157 See Julian Bond, "Civil Rights in the Popular Culture," *Southern Changes* 14, no. 2 (1992): 4, http://southernchanges.digitalscholarship.emory.edu/sc14-2_1204/sc14-2_002/.

Sources of Illustrations

State troopers preventing Henry Hobdy and Dorothy Davis from entering Murphy High School, Mobile, Alabama, September 9, 1963. Originally published in the *Mobile Press-Register*. Courtesy of the Alabama Media Group Collection, Alabama Department of Archives and History.

30   *A Time to Speak*, Jackson, Mississippi. Pamphlet by Mississippians for Public Education. Courtesy of the Constance Curry Papers, Stuart A. Rose Manuscript, Archives, and Rare Book Library, Emory University.

31   Stamp out Mississippi-ism, Join NAACP, 1956. Photograph by Al Ravenna. Courtesy of the Library of Congress Prints and Photographs Division, loc.gov/pictures/item/99401448.

33   WSB-TV newsfilm clip of an interracial classroom, New Orleans, Louisiana, December 1, 1960. Video still by WSB-TV Atlanta. Courtesy of the Civil Rights Digital Library, Walter J. Brown Media Archives, University of Georgia.

34   US marshals escort Ruby Bridges, New Orleans, Louisiana, November 14, 1960. Courtesy of Wikimedia Commons. Public domain. Ruby Bridges and President Barack Obama, Washington, DC, July 15, 2011. Video still by Executive Office staff. Courtesy of Wikimedia Commons. Public domain.

36   First grade class of African American and white school children seated on the floor, Charlotte, North Carolina, February 21, 1973. Photograph by Warren K. Leffler. Courtesy of the Library of Congress Prints and Photographs Division, loc.gov/item/2011646494.

38   Clipping from *Southern School News*, Nashville, Tennessee, March 1961. Courtesy of the Southern School News Collection, Civil Rights Digital Library, University of Georgia. Public domain.

41   WSB-TV newsfilm clip of Harvey Gantt, Clemson, South Carolina, January 2, 1963. Video still by WSB-TV Atlanta. Courtesy of the Civil Rights Digital Library, Walter J. Brown Media Archives, University of Georgia.

43   Crowds pack into Henry Grady High School, Atlanta, Georgia, March 23, 1960. Originally published in the *Atlanta Journal-Constitution*. Courtesy of the *Atlanta Journal-Constitution* Photographic Archive, Georgia State University.

44   Cover of the Sibley report, April 28, 1960. Courtesy of the Beverly Long Papers, Stuart A. Rose Manuscript, Archives, and Rare Book Library, Emory University.

45   Grady High School admits its first African American students, Atlanta, Georgia, September 6, 1961. Photograph by Bill Wilson. Originally published in the *Atlanta Journal-Constitution*. Courtesy of the *Atlanta*

Journal-Constitution Photographic Archive, Georgia State University.

46 WSB-TV newsfilm clip of reporter Abe Gallman, Atlanta, Georgia, January 30, 1970. Video still by WSB-TV Atlanta. Courtesy of the Civil Rights Digital Library, Walter J. Brown Media Archives, University of Georgia.

48 *The Citizens' Council*, Jackson, Mississippi, May 1956. Courtesy of Archive.org. Public domain.

51 Horace T. Ward, shaking hands with A.T. Walden, Donald Hollowell, Atlanta, Georgia, 1970. Originally published in the *Atlanta Journal-Constitution*. Courtesy of the *Atlanta Journal-Constitution* Photographic Archive, Georgia State University.

52 Newspaper clipping from *Southern School News*, Nashville, Tennessee, May 1964. Courtesy of the *Southern School News* Collection, Civil Rights Digital Library, University of Georgia. Public domain.

54 Milton Friedman, 1977. Courtesy of the University Archives Photograph Collection, Pepperdine University Special Collections and University Archives.

56 African American students arriving, Little Rock, Arkansas, September 1958. Photograph by John T. Bledsoe. Courtesy of the Library of Congress Prints and Photographs Division, loc.gov/pictures/item/2003673955.

60 Page from *Can We Afford to Close Our Public Schools?*, December 1959. Courtesy of the Beverly Long Papers, Stuart A. Rose Manuscript, Archives, and Rare Book Library, Emory University.

62 13 Known Private Schools in Virginia Established since 1958 to Circumvent Desegregation, 1965. Chart by Edward H. Peeples. Courtesy of the Edward H. Peeples Prince Edward County Public Schools Collection, James Branch Cabell Library Special Collections and Archives, Virginia Commonwealth University.

65 South's Share of Nation's Private School Enrollment, 1910–2012. Graph by Steve Suitts. Originally published in *Race and Ethnicity in a New Era of Public Funding of Private Schools* (Southern Education Foundation, 2016). Courtesy of the Southern Education Foundation.

67 Prince Edward Academy, Farmville, Virginia, ca. 1962. Photograph by Edward H. Peeples. Courtesy of the Edward H. Peeples Prince Edward County Public Schools Collection, James Branch Cabell Library Special Collections and Archives, Virginia Commonwealth University.

70 Dr. Jerry Falwell holds a religious rally, Tallahassee, Florida, 1980. Photograph by Mark T. Foley. Courtesy of Wikimedia Commons. Public domain.

72 Claiborne Academy, Claiborne Parish, Louisiana, May 26, 2009.

Photograph by Billy Hathorn. Courtesy of Wikimedia Commons. Creative Commons license CC BY-SA 3.0.

74 Rally at state capitol protesting the admission of the "Little Rock Nine," Little Rock, Arkansas, August 20, 1959. Photograph by John T. Bledsoe. Courtesy of the Library of Congress Prints and Photographs Division, loc.gov/item/2009632339.

77 White Students in Virtual Segregation: The Extent Private Schools Exceed Public Schools, 2012. Map by Steve Suitts. Originally published in *Race and Ethnicity in a New Era of Public Funding of Private Schools*. Courtesy of the Southern Education Foundation.

81 Under-Representation of Students of Color in Private Schools, 2012. Map by Steve Suitts. Originally published in *Race and Ethnicity in a New Era of Public Funding of Private Schools*. Courtesy of the Southern Education Foundation.

82 Percentages of White School Children Attending "Exclusionary" Schools, 2012. Table by Steve Suitts. Originally published in *Race and Ethnicity in a New Era of Public Funding of Private Schools*. Courtesy of the Southern Education Foundation.

83 Predominance of White Students in "Exclusionary" Private Schools by Section of the United States, 2012. Graph by Steve Suitts. Originally published in *Race and Ethnicity in a New Era of Public Funding of Private Schools*. Courtesy of the Southern Education Foundation.

87 Linda Brown Smith, Ethel Louise Belton Brown, Harry Briggs Jr., and Spottswood Bolling Jr. during press conference at Hotel Americana, June 9, 1964. Photograph by Al Ravenna. Courtesy of the Library of Congress Prints and Photographs Division, loc.gov/pictures/item/95503560.

92 Children and adults picketing for school integration, West Point, Mississippi, ca. 1965. Courtesy of the General Photograph Collection, Mississippi State University Libraries.

93 Public school teachers and supporters picket outside Milwaukee Public Schools administration building, Milwaukee, Wisconsin, April 24, 2018. Photograph by Charles Edward Miller. Courtesy of Wikimedia Commons. Creative Commons license CC BY-SA 2.0.

95 School Choice Programs in the United States, 2019. Map by Steve Suitts. Courtesy of the Southern Education Foundation.

Index